ISBN: 0615788009
ISBN-13: 978-0615788005

CONTENTS

LEVEL 1

QUESTIONS

1. **Which of the following are primary factors that contribute to a golf club's swing weight?**

   A. Height of the golfer and mass of the clubhead
   B. Length of the shaft and mass of the clubhead
   C. Height of the golfer and length of the shaft
   D. Swing speed and swing velocity

2. **If 2 inches of length are added to a driver, the swing weight will be increased by how many points?**

   A. 3 points
   B. 6 points
   C. 9 points
   D. 12 points

3. **Which of the following is the measure of a golf club's moment of inertia at a particular point?**

   A. Swing balance
   B. Swing torque
   C. Swing weight
   D. Swing precision

4. **All but which of the following are among the five human variables that influence clubhead speed?**

   A. Clubface position
   B. Neuromuscular coordination
   C. Body flexibility
   D. Leverage

5. Which of the following grips is well suited for golfers with short fingers and weak grip strength?

A. Overlapping grip
B. Interlocking grip
C. Ten-finger grip
D. None of the above

6. Which of the following grips is well suited for golfers with large fingers and strong hands?

A. Overlapping grip
B. Interlocking grip
C. Ten-finger grip
D. None of the above

7. Dynamic balance is defined as which of the following?

A. Equilibrium balance
B. Balance with movement
C. Balance of the golf club
D. Perceived balance

8. Which of the following is/are correct regarding timing and tempo in the golf swing?

(1) Tempo is the sequence of movements.
(2) Timing is the rate of movement.

A. (1) only
B. (2) only
C. All of the above
D. None of the above

9. **Decreasing swing weight by wrapping lead tape around the butt of the shaft is called _____ and should be avoided.**

   A. Counterbalancing
   B. Balancing
   C. Resetting
   D. Reforming

10. **Which of the following describes a shaft's resistance to twisting along its longitudinal axis? It affects the angle of the clubface at impact.**

    A. Angular momentum
    B. Torque
    C. Inertia
    D. Coiling

11. **Which of the following describes the roundness of the clubface that compensates for off-center hits by moving the center of gravity?**

    A. Curvature
    B. Bulge
    C. Progression
    D. Bend

12. **For lie angle to be fitted properly, the golf club should be at rest.**

    True
    False

13. **Examples of in-swing principles include release, swing center, and impact.**

    True
    False

14. An upright swing plane will cause the ball to come off the clubface with a lower trajectory and a draw. A flatter swing plane will cause the ball to come off the clubface with a higher trajectory and a fade.

True
False

15. If the loft of a golf club is altered, the hosel set will also be altered but the face progression will not be affected.

True
False

16. Impact ½ inch off the center of the clubface will result in a _____ loss in carry distance.

A. 4%
B. 7%
C. 8%
D. 10%

17. Which of the following are among the factors that influence how far a golf ball will travel?

A. Angle of approach
B. Clubhead speed
C. Centeredness of contact
D. All of the above

18. Which of the following is the platform for balancing the torso and swinging arms during a golf swing?

A. Core
B. Spine
C. Legs
D. Abdomen

19. The primary motion used to develop power in the golf swing is _____.

    A. Rotation
    B. Acceleration
    C. Coiling
    D. Velocity

20. All but which of the following are among the basic fundamentals of gripping a golf club?

    A. Placement
    B. Posture
    C. Pressure
    D. Precision

21. To produce a high golf ball trajectory, the shaft should have a _____ flex point.

    A. Low
    B. Mid
    C. High

22. Which of the following describes the relationship between a shaft's flexibility and the amount of clubhead weight?

    A. Shaft flexibility and clubhead weight are directly related. Adding weight to a clubhead will make the shaft perform more flexible.
    B. Shaft flexibility and clubhead weight are inversely related. Adding weight to a clubhead will make the shaft perform less flexible.
    C. There is no direct relationship between shaft flexibility and clubhead weight.

23. Examples of pre-swing principles include setup, position, and connection.

True
False

24. Double-sided grip tape should _____ be counted as a build-up layer.

   A. Always
   B. Sometimes
   C. Never

25. Which of the following describes the relationship between a shaft's flex point and the ball flight produced by the golf swing?

   A. Flex point and ball flight are directly related. A high flex point produces a high ball flight.
   B. Flex point and ball flight are inversely related. A high flex point produces a low ball flight.
   C. There is no direct relationship between flex point and ball flight.

26. Which of the following describes the measure of the angle at which the clubface lies relative to a vertical face represented by the shaft?

   A. Lie
   B. Loft
   C. Precision
   D. Bounce

27. Which of the following describes the measure of the angle between the center of the shaft and a line tangent to the sole of the clubhead?

   A. Lie
   B. Loft
   C. Precision
   D. Bounce

28. **Which of the following is/are correct regarding the optimal playing length of a golf club?**

    (1) The optimal playing length of a golf club is the length that produces centeredness of contact.
    (2) The optimal playing length of a golf club is the length that provides the widest swing arc.

    A. (1) only
    B. (2) only
    C. All of the above
    D. None of the above

29. **Maximum clubhead speed is achieved by combining the _____ overall weight and the _____ swing weight that a golfer can reasonably assume.**

    A. Lightest, Lightest
    B. Heaviest, Heaviest
    C. Lightest, Heaviest
    D. Heaviest, Lightest

30. **Which of the following is/are correct regarding the relationship between the length of a golf club and its lie angle?**

    (1) The longer the club, the more upright its lie angle will be.
    (2) The shorter the club, the flatter its lie angle will be.

    A. (1) only
    B. (2) only
    C. All of the above
    D. None of the above

31. **Which of the following is/are correct regarding golf club components?**

    (1) Golf clubs have four components: clubhead, shaft, hosel, and grip.
    (2) If any single component of a golf club is altered, the playing characteristics of the remaining components will also be changed.

    A. (1) only
    B. (2) only
    C. All of the above
    D. None of the above

32. **Lie angle affects the direction the clubface is pointing and how the ball leaves the clubface.**

    True
    False

33. **For every ½ inch of length that is added to an iron, the club will play _____ more upright.**

    A. 1 degree
    B. 2 degrees
    C. 4 degrees
    D. 6 degrees

34. **Which of the following are among the factors that influence the direction a golf ball will travel?**

    A. Swing path
    B. Clubface position
    C. Both swing path and clubface position
    D. None of the above

35. Which of the following is/are correct regarding swing path?

    (1) A push slice is the result of an inside-to-out swing path with a square clubface.
    (2) A pull hook is the result of an outside-to-in swing path with a square clubface.

    A. (1) only
    B. (2) only
    C. All of the above
    D. None of the above

36. Which of the following describes the hand position used if the hands are rotated in a clockwise position on the golf club?

    A. Open face
    B. Square face
    C. Closed face

37. Which of the following describes prematurely releasing the wrist on the forward swing? As a result, the clubhead arrives at the ball before the hands and arms.

    A. Lagging
    B. Casting
    C. Bobbing
    D. Extending

38. The lever system is a measure of the steepness of descent of the clubhead's forward swing. It influences the trajectory and distance the ball will travel.

    True
    False

39. Centrifugal force pulls the clubhead outward and downward, causes the arms to extend, and makes the clubhead take a circular path during the downswing.

    True
    False

40. Regarding laws and preferences, laws are the level at which golf instructors most often work.

True
False

41. Is an inside takeaway a law, principle, or preference?

A. Law
B. Principle
C. Preference

42. Is centeredness of contact a law, principle, or preference?

A. Law
B. Principle
C. Preference

43. "Placement" refers to gripping the golf club the same way each time.

True
False

44. The ten-finger grip is often used by adult male golfers because it favors those with strong wrists and forearms.

True
False

45. The primary factors that affect the distance a golf ball will travel are clubhead speed, angle of approach, and path of swing.

True
False

46. A steeper angle of approach creates _____ backspin, _____ lift, and _____ distance.

A. More, Less, Less
B. More, More, Less
C. Less, More, Less
D. Less, Less, More

47. Golf ball flight laws include path, angle of approach, face, centeredness of contact, and speed.

True
False

48. Examples of in-swing principles include swing plane, length of arc, and timing.

True
False

49. Examples of pre-swing principles include grip, aim, and dynamic balance.

True
False

50. The positional swing concept is well suited for athletic players, long hitters, and those with low handicaps.

True
False

51. The flo-swing concept is well suited for beginners, less athletic players, and short hitters.

True
False

52. The majority of golf swings that produce superior results have the clubhead approaching the ball from the _____ of the impact area.

A. Inside
B. Outside
C. Center

53. Which of the following is/are correct regarding a golf swing's arc width and arc length?

(1) Arc width is the extension of the golf club away from the body.
(2) Arc length is how far back the golf club is swung.

A. (1) only
B. (2) only
C. All of the above
D. None of the above

54. How many swing weights are equivalent to ¼ ounce?

A. 2
B. 3
C. 4
D. 5

55. If an M58 grip is installed on a .600 shaft, the grip will measure slightly larger than _____ the men's standard size.

A. 1/16 inch
B. 1/32 inch
C. 1/64 inch
D. None of the above

56. The most commonly accepted method of adjusting swing weight is to add or remove weight from the grip.

True
False

57. If a golf club's lie is too upright, the ball will travel to the _____ off the clubface. If a golf club's lie is too flat, the ball will travel to the _____ off the clubface.

A. Left, Left
B. Right, Left
C. Left, Right
D. Right, Right

58. The angle of the sole of the golf club to the ground when the shaft is perpendicular to the ground and the face is square to the target is known as which of the following?

A. Lie
B. Loft
C. Sole inversion
D. Counterbalance

59. A low center of gravity on the clubface will produce a _____ trajectory ball flight. A high center of gravity on the clubface will produce a _____ trajectory ball flight.

A. Low, High
B. High, Low

60. Impact ¼ inch off the center of the clubface will result in a _____ yard loss in distance. Impact ¾ inch off the center of the clubface will result in a _____ yard loss in distance.

A. 3, 12
B. 12, 30
C. 3, 30
D. 12, 24

61. There are 12 possible combinations of swing paths and clubface angles.

True
False

62. The loft of a wood is measured at the centerline of the hosel.

True
False

63. The effective loft of a wood is determined by _____ the number of degrees the club is open from the original loft. Or it is determined by _____ the number of degrees the club is closed from the original loft.

A. Adding, Adding
B. Adding, Subtracting
C. Subtracting, Adding
D. Subtracting, Subtracting

64. **Which of the following is/are correct regarding laws, principles, and preferences of the golf swing?**

    (1) A principle has direct relation to, and influence on, a law.
    (2) A preference must directly relate to a principle in order to be valid.

    A. (1) only
    B. (2) only
    C. All of the above
    D. None of the above

65. **The in-swing principle of position has the greatest influence on the law of angle of approach.**

    True
    False

66. **Human physiology is the scientific study of human movement.**

    True
    False

67. **Which of the following is the connective tissue that limits a muscle's range of motion?**

    A. Tendon
    B. Ligament
    C. Cartilage
    D. Fiber

68. **Which of the following connect muscles to bones?**

    A. Tendon
    B. Ligament
    C. Cartilage
    D. Fiber

69. Which of the following connect bones to other bones to form a joint?

A. Tendon
B. Ligament
C. Cartilage
D. Fiber

70. Which of the following is flexible connective tissue found in areas of the body such as the joints between bones, the rib cage, elbows, and knees?

A. Tendon
B. Ligament
C. Cartilage
D. Fiber

71. The function of _____ is to produce force and cause motion.

A. Tissue
B. Fiber
C. Muscle
D. Cartilage

72. Which of the following is the science that studies the structure of the human body?

A. Kinesiology
B. Biology
C. Anatomy
D. Physiology

73. Which of the following describes a golfer's ability to integrate his or her senses with motor function to produce accurate and skilled movement?

A. Neuromuscular coordination
B. Agility
C. Perceived balance
D. Hand-eye coordination

74. **Which of the following refers to a muscle contraction in response to elasticity within the muscle? It provides automatic regulation of skeletal muscle length.**

    A. Stretch reflex
    B. Stretch control
    C. Nerve reflex
    D. Spinal reflex

75. **A golf cart is something you pull, a golf car is something you ride in.**

    True
    False

76. **Which of the following is the second largest source of income for a golf facility behind playing fees?**

    A. Food and beverage operation
    B. Lessons
    C. Social events
    D. Golf cars

77. **According to the national average, a golf car rental should generate approximately _____ income per year for a golf facility.**

    A. $500
    B. $900
    C. $1,900
    D. $2,400

78. **Which of the following are among the responsibilities of the golf car fleet manager?**

    A. Maintenance, repair, and storage
    B. Golf car acquisition
    C. Developing golf car policies and procedures
    D. All of the above

79. The four physical characteristics of a golf course that affect the golf car fleet requirements are terrain, weather, paths, and yardage.

True
False

80. The national average golf car fleet size is _____ cars per golf facility.

A. 47
B. 57
C. 66
D. 76

81. Guidelines for estimating the size of a golf car fleet include 1 car per _____ playing members, and 1 car per _____ rounds of golf played annually.

A. 6, 600
B. 8, 800
C. 10, 1,000
D. 12, 1,200

82. Over half of all golf cars currently in use are _____.

A. Electric powered
B. Gas powered

83. Which of the following is/are correct regarding revenues and expenses attributed to golf cars?

(1) Golf car revenues are generated from rental fees, acquisition costs, number of cars, trade-in value, and storage costs.
(2) Golf car expenses are due to operating expenses, trail fees from private cars, car path costs, and trade-in value.

A. (1) only
B. (2) only
C. All of the above
D. None of the above

84. Calculate the expected annual golf car revenue for a golf facility that has 45 golf cars in operation, and each golf car is expected to complete 175 loops this year. Assume the golf car rental fee is $18 per round.

    A. $7,875
    B. $70,875
    C. $126,000
    D. $141,750

85. Calculate the expected annual golf car revenue for a golf facility that has 25,000 annual rounds played. Assume that 20% of all rounds include a golf car, and the golf car rental fee is $15 per round.

    A. $50,000
    B. $75,000
    C. $150,000
    D. $375,000

86. In general, _____ a golf car is better from a cash flow perspective. _____ a golf car results in more equity.

    A. Leasing, Leasing
    B. Leasing, Purchasing
    C. Purchasing, Leasing
    D. Purchasing, Purchasing

87. Which type of golf car lease requires the lessee to pay the same amount each month, and the lessor is responsible for providing parts and services?

    A. Full maintenance fixed rate lease
    B. Skip payment lease
    C. Escalating lease
    D. Lease purchase

88. Which type of golf car lease does not require payments during the off-season?

A. Full maintenance fixed rate lease
B. Skip payment lease
C. Escalating lease
D. Lease purchase

89. What percentage of private and daily fee courses require golf cars at least part of the year?

A. 20%
B. 30%
C. 50%
D. 60%

90. Adequate record keeping for a golf car fleet includes maintaining financing, rotation, and maintenance records.

True
False

91. The national average rental fee for a golf car is between $25 and $30 per round.

True
False

92. Possible methods of financing golf car acquisitions include the PGA credit union, banks, and commercial finance corporations.

True
False

93. It is not necessary to notify the insurance company following a golf car accident because golf cars are not considered passenger vehicles.

True
False

94. Which of the following are the two main categories of golf car maintenance?

A. Preventative maintenance and repair
B. Cleaning and repair
C. Preventative maintenance and rotation
D. Rotation and repair

95. Adequate storage space for a golf car is _____ square feet per car.

A. 20 to 25
B. 30 to 35
C. 50 to 55
D. 70 to 75

96. The USGA Rules Committee is responsible for developing the language for a proposed rule change.

True
False

97. Which sections of the Rules of Golf contain rules regarding a ball that is lost, out of bounds, or unplayable?

A. Rules 7-8
B. Rules 13-15
C. Rules 18-19
D. Rules 27-28

98. Which sections of the Rules of Golf communicate rules associated with match play and stroke play competition?

    A. Rules 2-3
    B. Rules 5-6
    C. Rules 11-12
    D. Rules 24-25

99. The original Rules of Golf were in created in which of the following years?

    A. 1698
    B. 1744
    C. 1837
    D. 1916

100. When the original Rules of Golf were created, how many rules were initially implemented?

    A. 7 rules
    B. 9 rules
    C. 11 rules
    D. 13 rules

101. The Royal and Ancient Golf Club (R&A) became the governing world authority for the Rules of Golf in which of the following years?

    A. 1844
    B. 1897
    C. 1916
    D. 1927

102. Which of the following groups was formed in the year 1894?

    A. Royal and Ancient Golf Club (R&A)
    B. United States Golf Association (USGA)
    C. International Association of Golf Administrators (IAGA)
    D. PGA of America

103. **Changes may be made to the Rules of Golf every _____ years. Changes may be made to the Decisions on the Rules of Golf every _____ years.**

    A. 3, 2
    B. 2, 4
    C. 4, 2
    D. 2, 3

104. **Which of the following may be moved without unreasonable effort or delaying play, and without damage?**

    A. Movable obstructions
    B. Immovable obstructions

105. **An obstruction is deemed to be _____ if it takes reasonable effort to move, or causes delays in play.**

    A. Movable
    B. Immovable

106. **Which of the following markings may be used to identify ground under repair?**

    A. White stakes only
    B. Orange lines only
    C. White stakes or orange lines
    D. None of the above

107. **"Through the green" is the whole area of the golf course including the teeing area and putting green of the hole being played, and all hazards on the course.**

    True
    False

108. **Loose impediments exclude items that are fixed, growing, embedded, or adhering to the ball.**

True
False

109. **Snow and natural ice located on a golf course are considered which of the following?**

A. Casual water only
B. Loose impediments only
C. Casual water or loose impediments
D. None of the above

110. **Loose impediments include natural objects found on a golf course, such as stones, twigs, worms, and insects.**

True
False

111. **Which of the following markings may be used to identify a water hazard?**

A. Yellow stakes only
B. White lines only
C. Yellow lines only
D. Yellow stakes or yellow lines

112. **Which of the following is/are correct regarding water hazards and ground under repair?**

(1) A ball is considered to be in ground under repair if the entire ball is inside the line.
(2) A ball is considered to be in a water hazard if any part of the ball touches the hazard.

A. (1) only
B. (2) only
C. All of the above
D. None of the above

113. Which of the following are relief options from a water hazard?

    A. Play the ball as it lies.
    B. Play the ball as near as possible from where it was last played.
    C. Drop the ball on an extended line between the flagstick and where the ball last crossed the hazard.
    D. All of the above are relief options from a water hazard.

114. Which of the following is/are correct regarding relief options from a lateral water hazard?

    (1) Drop the ball at a point equidistant from where the ball last crossed the hazard, no nearer to the hole.
    (2) Drop the ball one club length from the point where the ball last crossed the hazard, no nearer to the hole.

    A. (1) only
    B. (2) only
    C. All of the above
    D. None of the above

115. The Rules of Golf contain 34 rules, 47 definitions, and 3 appendices.

    True
    False

116. The USGA and R&A have carefully coordinated rules, and the two bodies have always held the same rules at the same time.

    True
    False

117. In 1920, the **USGA** and **R&A** agreed that golf balls shall weigh a maximum of _____ ounces, and have a maximum diameter of _____ inches.

    A. 1.22, 2.10
    B. 1.48, 1.82
    C. 1.62, 1.68
    D. 2.00, 2.30

118. The penalty in stroke play for a rule violation is 1 stroke unless otherwise noted.

    True
    False

119. The penalty in match play for a rule violation is 2 strokes unless otherwise noted.

    True
    False

120. The **PGA** of America was founded in which of the following years?

    A. 1844
    B. 1897
    C. 1916
    D. 1923

121. How many articles define the **PGA Constitution**?

    A. 4
    B. 5
    C. 6
    D. 7

122. Which of the following **PGA Constitution** articles is paired with the correct description?

    (1) Article 1: Name and Purpose
    (2) Article 2: Organization

    A. (1) only
    B. (2) only
    C. All of the above
    D. None of the above

123. Which of the following **PGA Constitution** articles is paired with the correct description?

    (1) Article 3: PGA Tour
    (2) Article 4: Meetings

    A. (1) only
    B. (2) only
    C. All of the above
    D. None of the above

124. Which of the following outline the general philosophies, practices, and procedures of the **PGA Constitution**, as agreed upon by the **Association**?

    A. Articles
    B. Regulations
    C. Bylaws
    D. None of the above

125. Which of the following explain the Bylaws of the **PGA Constitution**?

    A. Articles
    B. Regulations
    C. Appendix
    D. None of the above

126. According to the **PGA Constitution**, the **President** serves as the **Chairman of the Board**, presides at all meetings, and is the spokesman for the **Association**.

    True
    False

127. According to the **PGA Constitution**, the **Vice President** is responsible for managing all membership matters for the **Association**, and serves as the **Chairperson of the Board of Control**.

    True
    False

128. According to the **PGA Constitution**, the **Secretary** is responsible for managing all financial matters for the **Association**.

    True
    False

129. According to the **PGA Constitution**, how many members make up the **Board of Directors?**

    A. 13
    B. 17
    C. 21
    D. 25

130. To be recognized by the **PGA**, a 9-hole golf course must be at least _____ yards in length, and an 18-hole golf course must be at least _____ yards in length.

    A. 1,000, 1,500
    B. 1,500, 3,000
    C. 2,000, 3,000
    D. 2,000, 4,000

131. **A PGA** recognized golf course must have at least _____ acres in total course area, exclusive of the clubhouse, golf shop, and parking areas.

   A. 10
   B. 14
   C. 18
   D. 22

132. It is not necessary that a **PGA** recognized golf range have a **PGA Professional** available for instruction.

   True
   False

133. **A PGA** recognized golf range must have a minimum of _____ tees and _____ feet of teeing area.

   A. 6, 60
   B. 9, 90
   C. 12, 120
   D. 15, 150

134. **An Assistant PGA Professional** must spend at least _____ of his or her time working on tournament operations, golf car operations, staff scheduling, bookkeeping, merchandising, club repair, and handicapping records.

   A. 33%
   B. 50%
   C. 66%
   D. 75%

135. **The Director of Golf** directs the total golf operation, including the golf shop, golf range, and golf car fleet.

   True
   False

136. According to the **PGA Constitution**, the penalty for an ethics violation may include which of the following?

   A. Monetary fines up to $5,000
   B. Loss of playing privileges in national events only
   C. Suspension or expulsion from the PGA
   D. All of the above

137. The **PGA Board of Control** meets quarterly and reviews all membership matters.

   True
   False

138. In order to become a **PGA Section**, there must be at least _____ **PGA** Professionals within a _____ mile radius.

   A. 25, 50
   B. 50, 140
   C. 100, 200
   D. 150, 240

139. Which of the following are among the requirements to become a **PGA Apprentice?**

   A. Must be endorsed by a PGA member
   B. Pass the Playing Ability Test
   C. Be eligibly employed for at least 6 months
   D. All of the above are required to become a PGA Apprentice.

140. Which of the following individuals is responsible for recruiting, hiring, training, and supervising all staff including teaching professionals, outside assistants, mechanics, starters, and rangers?

   A. Head Professional
   B. General Manager
   C. The Head Professional and General Manager share these duties.
   D. None of the above

141. Which of the following individuals oversee tee times, starting, handicapping, and all other golf services?

A. Head Professional
B. General Manager
C. The Head Professional and General Manager share these duties.
D. None of the above

142. Which of the following individuals oversee all aspects of the facility including its activities and the relationships between the facility, its patrons, employees, community, government, and industry?

A. Head Professional
B. General Manager
C. The Head Professional and General Manager share these duties.
D. None of the above

143. Which of the following individuals is responsible for developing the annual business plan, implementing general policies and procedures, and maintaining a sound organizational structure?

A. Head Professional
B. General Manager
C. The Head Professional and General Manager share these duties.
D. None of the above

144. According to the PGA Constitution, if a PGA Professional commits a rule violation, possible punishments may include all but which of the following?

A. Counseling
B. Probation
C. Reprimand
D. Expulsion

145. The officers of the PGA include all but which of the following?

    A. President
    B. Vice President
    C. Treasurer
    D. Secretary

146. The PGA has _____ districts and _____ sections.

    A. 6, 18
    B. 8, 36
    C. 9, 40
    D. 14, 41

147. The mission of The PGA of America is to promote the enjoyment and involvement of the game of golf, and to contribute to its growth by providing services to golf professionals, consumers, and the golf industry.

    True
    False

148. All but which of the following are rights entitled to PGA members?

    A. The right to vote
    B. The right to hold office
    C. The right to use the PGA name and logo
    D. All of the above are rights entitled to PGA members.

149. In order for a PGA Professional to maintain active membership status, he or she must achieve a minimum amount of professional development points to be earned in a 3-year period, as determined by the Board of Directors.

    True
    False

150. All members of the PGA Board of Directors must be either past national officers, past national directors, or past section leaders.

    True
    False

151. For a match play event with 16 ordered qualifiers, the number 5 qualifier's opening match will be played against the number _____ qualifier.

    A. 8
    B. 10
    C. 12
    D. 14

152. Tee markers should be placed _____ yards apart in the teeing area.

    A. 4
    B. 5
    C. 6
    D. 8

153. All but which of the following are typically listed on a tournament pairing sheet?

    A. Tournament officials
    B. Handicaps
    C. Format of event
    D. All of the above are listed on a pairing sheet.

154. At the conclusion of a tournament round, a competitor submits a scorecard with a gross score of 77. Each individual hole-by-hole score is correct, but when added by the committee the total score is 78. What is the competitor's official score?

    A. 77
    B. 78
    C. 80
    D. The competitor is disqualified.

155. The _____ handicap system matches a competitor's net score to a randomly selected number between 70 and 90.

    A. Wilson
    B. Blind Bogey
    C. Peoria
    D. Callaway

156. The _____ handicap system deducts a number of the worst hole scores from the combined score of the first 16 holes.

    A. Wilson
    B. Blind Bogey
    C. Peoria
    D. Callaway

157. All but which of the following are parts of the **PGA Teaching Triangle**?

    A. How
    B. What
    C. Where
    D. When

158. All but which of the following are popular forms of learning the golf swing?

    A. Verbal
    B. Visual
    C. Kinesthetic
    D. These are all popular forms of learning the golf swing.

159. The four parts of the basic golf swing learning model are establish, gather, analyze, and implement.

    True
    False

160. The three functions of a golf instructor providing feedback to a student are to fix an error, provide motivation, and serve as reinforcement.

    True
    False

161. When an instructor and student are developing goals, they should select goals that are broad in nature. For example, a goal should not be, "Become a 10-handicap by Labor Day."

    True
    False

162. The _____ is a single error the student makes that causes additional errors to be made. The _____ is to fix the central error because it will help fix other errors as well.

    A. Critical error, Critical key
    B. Critical error, Master key
    C. Master error, Critical key
    D. Master error, Master key

163. A golf professional's employment contract may include a provision that provides an annual cost of living increase correlated with the Consumer Price Index (CPI). What is this provision called?

    A. CPI rider
    B. Inflation adjustment
    C. Codicil
    D. Amendment to the contract

164. All but which of the following are correct regarding the arbitration process?

    A. Arbitration can be either voluntary or mandatory, and binding or non-binding.
    B. Arbitration is less expensive than litigation.
    C. Arbitration is less time consuming than litigation.
    D. All of the above are correct regarding the arbitration process.

165. Which of the following describes an arrangement in which a portion of the golf professional's income is paid out at a date after which the income is actually earned? Examples include pensions, retirement plans, and stock options.

    A. Non-qualified compensation
    B. Defined contribution plan
    C. Deferred compensation
    D. Group carve-out plan

166. Which of the following clauses found in an employment contract explains what will happen to a golf professional if his or her golf facility is bought or merged with another?

    A. Indemnification clause
    B. Arbitration clause
    C. Severability clause
    D. Merger clause

167. All but which of the following are key elements found in an employment agreement?

    A. Duties and responsibilities of the employer
    B. Policies on time off
    C. Indemnification clause
    D. Termination clause

168. Employment contracts may specify that in the event of any controversy or claim arising from the contract, the matter will be subject to arbitration.

    True
    False

169. An _____ clause found in an employment contract provides an automatic annual extension of the contract as long as neither party notifies the other that they wish to terminate the agreement.

    A. Indemnity
    B. Evergreen
    C. Acceptance
    D. Integration

170. A typical long-term disability insurance policy will pay a disabled employee a maximum benefit of _____ of his or her pre-disability income.

    A. 50% to 75%
    B. 60% to 66%
    C. 90% to 100%
    D. 35% to 40%

171. Which of the following are non-taxable fringe benefits a PGA Professional may receive as part of his or her compensation package?

    A. Season tickets to a sporting event
    B. Personal use of company car, airplane, or lodging
    C. Use of employer-provided on-premise athletic facilities
    D. Country club dues paid by an employer on behalf of an employee

172. Free meals and lodging provided to a PGA Professional for the employer's convenience are non-taxable fringe benefits.

    True
    False

173. According to the **US Department of Labor Child Labor Rules,** 14- and 15-year-old minors may work no more than _____ hours on a school day, and _____ hours on a non-school day.

A. 3, 8
B. 5, 8
C. 3, 6
D. 4, 7

174. According to the **US Department of Labor Child Labor Rules,** 14- and 15-year-old minors may work no more than _____ hours per week when school is in session, and _____ hours per week when school is not in session.

A. 10, 20
B. 20, 36
C. 12, 30
D. 18, 40

175. According to the **US Department of Labor Child Labor Rules,** 14- and 15-year-old minors may not work before 8:00 am or after 8:00 pm.

True
False

176. Which of the following **Acts** established a national minimum wage and set overtime pay requirements?

A. Fair Labor Standards Act of 1938
B. Fair Labor Standards Act of 1961
C. Contract Work Hours Standards Act
D. Equal Pay Act of 1963

177. Tony has been employed by The Golf Club for three years. He is an Assistant PGA Professional and earns an annual salary of $50,000. Tiffany has also been employed by The Golf Club for the same length of time, and shares the same job description, but she earns a salary of only $45,000. Which of the following Acts might The Golf Club be in violation of?

    A. Fair Labor Standards Act of 1938
    B. Fair Labor Standards Act of 1961
    C. Contract Work Hours Standards Act
    D. Equal Pay Act of 1963

178. Which of the following requires employers to provide employees with a safe and healthy work environment?

    A. OSHA
    B. FLSA
    C. ERISA
    D. ADEA

179. Which of the following requires retirement plans to provide participants with important information about plan features and funding?

    A. OSHA
    B. FLSA
    C. ERISA
    D. ADEA

180. Which of the following requires employers to verify the identity and work status of each new employee the company hires?

    A. OSHA
    B. EPPA
    C. ERISA
    D. IRCA

181. **The Veterans Rights and Military Service Act requires companies to rehire employees who were called to, or volunteered for, military service.**

    True
    False

182. **According to workers compensation laws, a court order is required in order to have an employer withhold a specific amount of money from an employee's wage for payment of a debt to a third party. For example, child support, bankruptcy, or unpaid taxes.**

    True
    False

183. **The Age Discrimination in Employment Act (ADEA) prohibits employers from discriminating against workers who are older than age _____.**

    A. 18
    B. 21
    C. 30
    D. 40

184. **The Civil Rights Act states that it is illegal for a company to decide not to hire an applicant for a position because of the applicant's gender, race, or religion.**

    True
    False

185. **The Equal Pay Act requires equal pay for equal work, regardless of sex.**

    True
    False

186. The Americans with Disabilities Act (ADA) prohibits an employer from discriminating against a qualified disabled worker, even if the disabled worker is unable to perform all of the duties required for the job.

    True
    False

187. The Fair Labor Standards Act is concerned with all but which of the following areas of employment?

    A. Hiring practices
    B. Record keeping
    C. Overtime pay
    D. Child labor standards

188. According to Federal Wage and Hour laws, a golf professional's overtime pay is required to be which of the following?

    A. Time and a half
    B. Hourly wage times two
    C. Hourly wage times three
    D. Any of the above are permitted.

189. Employers who have _____ or more employees are subject to COBRA rules.

    A. 18
    B. 20
    C. 25
    D. 30

190. COBRA coverage is limited to _____ months for employees, and _____ months for dependents of employees.

    A. 6, 12
    B. 12, 24
    C. 9, 18
    D. 18, 36

191. According to the Truth in Lending Act (TILA), if an employer would like to conduct a background check or credit check on an applicant, they must inform the applicant in writing.

True
False

192. All but which of the following are among the employment services provided by the PGA?

A. Career Net
B. Career Links
C. Career Chips
D. Career Partners

193. Which of the following is an online job posting service that helps PGA Head Professionals hire assistants and other staff?

A. Career Net
B. Career Links
C. Career Chips
D. Career Partners

194. All but which of the following are basic types of résumés?

A. Functional
B. Traditional
C. Targeted
D. Chronological

195. Which type of résumé is most commonly used to apply for job openings in the golf industry?

A. Functional
B. Traditional
C. Targeted
D. Chronological

196. All but which of the following should be included on a résumé?

A. Community service
B. Military service
C. Extracurricular activities
D. All of the above should be included on a résumé.

197. Which of the following should be included on a résumé?

A. Religious affiliations
B. Professional affiliations
C. Social affiliations
D. All of the above should be included on a résumé.

198. Which of the following should be avoided when a golf professional is networking via telephone?

A. Asking for a job
B. Asking for information about the facility
C. Asking for the names of decision makers at the facility
D. All of the above should be avoided when networking via telephone.

199. Which of the following is correct regarding the relationship between golf professionals and golf facilities in today's golf industry?

A. There are currently more golf facilities than trained golf professionals.
B. There are currently more trained golf professionals than golf facilities.
C. There is an equal number of trained golf professionals and golf facilities.
D. The relationship cannot be determined.

200. There are approximately 45,000 men and women PGA Professionals and PGA Apprentices.

True
False

ANSWER KEY

1. B

The two primary factors that contribute to a golf club's swing weight are the length of the shaft and the mass of the clubhead.

2. D

For every 1 inch of length that is added to a driver, the swing weight will increase by 6 points. Therefore, if 2 inches of length are added to a driver, the swing weight will increase by 12 points.

3. C

Swing weight is the measure of a golf club's moment of inertia at a particular point.

4. A

The five human variables that influence clubhead speed are neuromuscular coordination, body flexibility, leverage, swing technique, and physical strength.

5. B

The interlocking grip is well suited for golfers with short fingers and weak grip strength.

6. A

The overlapping grip is well suited for golfers with large fingers and short hands.

7. B

Dynamic balance is defined as balance with movement.

8. D

Timing is the sequence of movements. Tempo is the rate of movement.

9. A

Decreasing swing weight by wrapping lead tape around the butt of the shaft is called counterbalancing and should be avoided.

10. B

Torque is a shaft's resistance to twisting along its longitudinal axis. It affects the angle of the clubface at impact.

11. B
The roundness of the clubface that compensates for off-center hits by moving the center of gravity is known as bulge.

12. False
Lie angle should be fitted dynamically, meaning the club fitter should examine the lie angle when the club is impacting the ball.

13. True
Examples of in-swing principles include release, swing center, and impact.

14. False
A flatter swing plane will cause the ball to come off the clubface with a lower trajectory and a draw. An upright swing plane will cause the ball to come off the clubface with a higher trajectory and a fade.

15. False
If the loft of a golf club is altered, the hosel set and face progression will also be changed.

16. B
Impact ½ inch off the center of the clubface will result in a 7% loss in carry distance.

17. D
The factors that influence how far a golf ball with travel are angle of approach, clubhead speed, and centeredness of contact.

18. C
The legs are the platform for balancing the torso and swinging arms during a golf swing.

19. A
The primary motion used to develop power in the golf swing is rotation.

20. B
The basic fundamentals of gripping a golf club are placement, pressure, precision, and position.

21. A
To produce a high golf ball trajectory, the shaft should have a low flex point.

22. A
Shaft flexibility and clubhead weight are directly related. Adding weight to a clubhead will make the shaft perform more flexible.

23. False

Examples of pre-swing principles include grip, aim, and setup. Position and connection are in-swing principles.

24. C

Double-sided grip tape should never be counted as a build-up layer.

25. B

Flex point and ball flight are inversely related. A high flex point produces a low ball flight.

26. B

Loft is the measure of the angle at which the clubface lies relative to a vertical face represented by the shaft.

27. A

Lie is the measure of the angle between the center of the shaft and a line tangent to the sole of the clubhead.

28. A

The optimal playing length of a golf club is the length that produces centeredness of contact.

29. C

Maximum clubhead speed is achieved by combining the lightest overall weight and the heaviest swing weight that a golfer can reasonably assume.

30. D

The shorter the club, the more upright its lie angle will be. The longer the club, the flatter its lie angle will be.

31. B

Golf clubs have three components: clubhead, shaft, and grip. If any single component of a golf club is altered, the playing characteristics of the remaining components will also be changed.

32. True

Lie angle affects the direction the clubface is pointing and how the ball leaves the clubface.

33. A

For every ½ inch of length that is added to an iron, the club will play 1 degree more upright.

34. C

The primary factors that influence the direction a golf ball will travel are swing path and clubface position.

35. D

Neither statement regarding swing path is correct.

36. C

A closed face hand position results when the hands are rotated in a clockwise position on the golf club.

37. B

Casting is prematurely releasing the wrist on the forward swing. As a result, the clubhead arrives at the ball before the hands and arms.

38. False

The angle of approach is a measure of the steepness of descent of the clubhead's forward swing. It influences the trajectory and distance the ball will travel.

39. True

Centrifugal force pulls the clubhead outward and downward, causes the arms to extend, and makes the clubhead take a circular path during the downswing.

40. False

Preferences are the level at which golf instructors most often work.

41. C

An inside takeaway is a preference.

42. A

Centeredness of contact is a law.

43. False

Precision refers to gripping the golf club the same way each time.

44. False

The overlapping grip is often used by adult male golfers because it favors those with strong wrists and forearms.

45. False

The primary factors that affect the distance a golf ball will travel are clubhead speed, angle of approach, and centeredness of contact.

46. B

A steeper angle of approach creates more backspin, more lift, and less distance.

47. True

Golf ball flight laws include path, angle of approach, face, centeredness of contact, and speed.

48. True

Examples of in-swing principles include swing plane, length of arc, and timing.

49. False

Examples of pre-swing principles include grip, aim, and setup. Dynamic balance is an example of an in-swing principle.

50. True

The positional swing concept is well suited for athletic players, long hitters, and those with low handicaps.

51. True

The flo-swing concept is well suited for beginners, less athletic players, and short hitters.

52. A

The majority of golf swings that produce superior results have the clubhead approaching the ball from the inside of the impact area.

53. C

Arc width is the extension of the golf club away from the body. Arc length is how far back the golf club is swung.

54. C

Four swing weights are equivalent to ¼ ounce.

55. C

If an M58 grip is installed on a .600 shaft, the grip will measure slightly larger than 1/64" the men's standard size.

56. False
The most commonly accepted method of adjusting swing weight is to add or remove weight from the clubhead.

57. C
If a golf club's lie is too upright, the ball will travel to the left off the clubface. If a golf club's lie is too flat, the ball will travel to the right off the clubface.

58. C
Sole inversion is defined as the angle of the sole of the golf club to the ground when the shaft is perpendicular to the ground and the face is square to the target.

59. B
A low center of gravity on the clubface will produce a high trajectory ball flight. A high center of gravity on the clubface will produce a low trajectory ball flight.

60. C
Impact ¼ inch off the center of the clubface will result in a 3 yard loss in distance. Impact ¾ inch off the center of the clubface will result in a 30 yard loss in distance.

61. False
There are 9 possible combinations of swing paths and clubface angles.

62. False
The loft of a wood is measured at a point half the distance of the face height on the centerline of the face.

63. C
The effective loft of a wood is determined by subtracting the number of degrees the club is open from the original loft. Or it is determined by adding the number of degrees the club is closed from the original loft.

64. C
A principle has direct relation to, and influence on, a law. A preference must directly relate to a principle in order to be valid.

65. False
The in-swing principle of position has the greatest influence on the law of face.

66. False

Kinesiology is the scientific study of human movement.

67. B

A ligament is connective tissue that limits a muscle's range of motion.

68. A

Tendons connect muscles to bones.

69. B

Ligaments connect bones to other bones to form a joint.

70. C

Cartilage is flexible connective tissue found in areas of the body such as the joints between bones, the rib cage, elbows, and knees.

71. C

The function of muscle is to produce force and cause motion.

72. C

Anatomy is the science that studies the structure of the human body.

73. A

Neuromuscular coordination describes a golfer's ability to integrate his or her senses with motor function to produce accurate and skilled movement.

74. A

Stretch reflex refers to a muscle contraction in response to elasticity within the muscle. It provides automatic regulation of skeletal muscle length.

75. True

A golf cart is something you pull, a golf car is something you ride in.

76. D

Golf cars are the second largest source of income for a golf facility behind playing fees.

77. C

According to the national average, a golf car rental should generate approximately $1,900 income per year for a golf facility.

78. D
The responsibilities of the golf car fleet manager include maintenance, repair, storage, golf car acquisition, and developing operating policies and procedures.

79. True
The four physical characteristics of a golf course that affect the golf car fleet requirements are terrain, weather, paths, and yardage.

80. B
The national average golf car fleet size is 57 cars per golf facility.

81. B
Guidelines for estimating the size of a golf car fleet include 1 car per 8 playing members, and 1 car per 800 rounds of golf played annually.

82. A
Over half of all golf cars currently in use are electric powered.

83. D
Golf car revenues are generated from rental fees, car rounds, number of cars, trade-in value, and trail fees from private cars. Golf car expenses are due to operating expenses, acquisition costs, car path costs, and storage costs.

84. D
45 golf cars x 175 loops x $18 per round = $141,750 revenue

85. B
25,000 x 20% = 5,000
5,000 x $15 = $75,000

86. B
In general, leasing a golf car is better from a cash flow perspective. Purchasing a golf car results in more equity.

87. A
A full maintenance fixed rate lease requires the lessee to pay the same amount each month, and the lessor is responsible for providing parts and services.

88. B

A skip payment lease does not require payments during the off-season.

89. B

30% of private and daily fee courses require golf cars at least part of the year.

90. True

Adequate record keeping for a golf car fleet includes maintaining financing, rotation, and maintenance records.

91. False

The national average rental fee for a golf car is between $14 and $18 per round.

92. True

Possible methods of financing golf car acquisitions include the PGA credit union, banks, and commercial finance corporations.

93. False

It is necessary to notify the insurance company immediately following a golf car accident, even if the accident is minor.

94. A

The two main categories of golf car maintenance are preventative maintenance and repair.

95. D

Adequate storage space for a golf car is 70 to 75 square feet per car.

96. False

The Rules Drafting Committee is responsible for developing the language for a proposed rule change.

97. D

Rules 27-28 contain rules regarding a ball that is lost, out of bounds, or unplayable.

98. A

Rules 2-3 communicate rules associated with match play and stroke play competition.

99. B

The original Rules of Golf were created in the year 1744.

100. D
The original Rules of Golf contained 13 rules.

101. B
The Royal and Ancient Golf Club (R&A) became the governing world authority for the Rules of Golf in the year 1897.

102. B
The United States Golf Association (USGA) was formed in the year 1894.

103. C
Changes may be made to the Rules of Golf every 4 years. Changes may be made to the Decisions on the Rules of Golf every 2 years.

104. A
Movable obstructions may be moved without unreasonable effort or delaying play, and without damage.

105. B
An obstruction is deemed to be immovable if it takes reasonable effort to move, or causes delays in play.

106. D
Orange stakes or white lines may be used to identify ground under repair.

107. False
"Through the green" is the whole area of the golf course except the teeing area and putting green of the hole being played, and all hazards on the course.

108. True
Loose impediments exclude items that are fixed, growing, embedded, or adhering to the ball.

109. C
Snow and natural ice located on a golf course are considered either casual water or loose impediments.

110. True
Loose impediments include natural objects found on a golf course, such as stones, twigs, worms, and insects.

111. D
Yellow stakes or yellow lines may be used to identify a water hazard.

112. B
A ball is considered to be in ground under repair if any part of the ball touches the line. A ball is considered to be in a water hazard if any part of the ball touches the hazard.

113. D
Relief options from a water hazard include:
(1) Play the ball as it lies.
(2) Play the ball as near as possible from where it was last played.
(3) Drop the ball on an extended line between the flagstick and where the ball last crossed the hazard.

114. A
Relief options from a lateral water hazard include:
(1) Drop the ball at a point equidistant from where the ball last crossed the hazard, no nearer to the hole.
(2) Drop the ball two club lengths from the point where the ball last crossed the hazard, no nearer to the hole.

115. True
The Rules of Golf contain 34 rules, 47 definitions, and 3 appendices.

116. False
The USGA and the R&A have not always held the same rules.

117. C
In 1920, the USGA and R&A agreed that golf balls shall weigh a maximum of 1.62 ounces, and have a maximum diameter of 1.68 inches.

118. False
The penalty in stroke play for a rule violation is 2 strokes unless otherwise noted.

119. False
The penalty in match play for a rule violation is loss of hole.

120. C
The PGA of America was founded in the year 1916.

121. B
Five articles define the PGA Constitution.

122. A
Article 1: Name and Purpose
Article 2: Membership

123. B
Article 3: Organization
Article 4: Meetings

124. C
Bylaws outline the general philosophies, practices, and procedures of the PGA Constitution, as agreed upon by the Association.

125. B
Regulations explain the Bylaws of the PGA Constitution.

126. True
According to the PGA Constitution, the President serves as the Chairman of the Board, presides at all meetings, and is the spokesman for the Association.

127. False
According to the PGA Constitution, the Vice President is responsible for managing all financial matters for the Association.

128. False
According to the PGA Constitution, the Secretary is responsible for managing all membership matters for the Association, and serves as the Chairperson of the Board of Control.

129. C
According to the PGA Constitution, 21 members make up the Board of Directors.

130. A
To be recognized by the PGA, a 9-hole golf course must be at least 1,000 yards in length, and an 18-hole golf course must be at least 1,500 yards in length.

131. B
A PGA recognized golf course must have at least 14 acres in total course area, exclusive of the clubhouse, golf shop, and parking areas.

132. False

A PGA Professional must be available for instruction at a PGA recognized golf range.

133. D

A PGA recognized golf range must have a minimum of 15 tees and 150 feet of teeing area.

134. B

An Assistant PGA Professional must spend at least 50% of his or her time working on tournament operations, golf car operations, staff scheduling, bookkeeping, merchandising, club repair, and handicapping records.

135. True

The Director of Golf directs the total golf operation, including the golf shop, golf range, and golf car fleet. The Director of Golf also supervises the Head Professional.

136. C

According to the PGA Constitution, the penalty for an ethics violation may include:
(1) Monetary fines up to $1,000
(2) Loss of playing privileges in sectional and national events
(3) Suspension or expulsion from the PGA

137. True

The PGA Board of Control meets quarterly and reviews all membership matters.

138. B

In order to become a PGA Section, there must be at least 50 PGA Professionals within a 140 mile radius.

139. D

All of the items listed are required to become a PGA Apprentice.

140. A

The Head Professional is responsible for recruiting, hiring, training, and supervising all staff including teaching professionals, outside assistants, mechanics, starters, and rangers.

141. A

The Head Professional oversees tee times, starting, handicapping, and all other golf services.

142. B

The General Manager oversees all aspects of the facility including its activities and the relationships between the facility, its patrons, employees, community, government, and industry.

143. B
The General Manager is responsible for developing the annual business plan, implementing general policies and procedures, and maintaining a sound organizational structure.

144. A
According to the PGA Constitution, if a PGA Professional commits a rule violation, possible punishments may include probation, reprimand, suspension, and expulsion.

145. C
The officers of the PGA are the President, Vice President, Secretary, and Honorary President.

146. D
The PGA has 14 districts and 41 sections.

147. True
The mission of The PGA of America is to promote the enjoyment and involvement of the game of golf, and to contribute to its growth by providing services to golf professionals, consumers, and the golf industry.

148. D
PGA members have the right to vote; the right to hold office; the right to use the PGA name and logo; and the right to attend annual meetings as an observer.

149. True
In order for a PGA Professional to maintain active membership status, he or she must achieve a minimum amount of professional development points to be earned in a 3-year period, as determined by the Board of Directors.

150. False
All members of the PGA Board of Control must be either past national officers, past national directors, or past section leaders.

151. C
For a match play event with 16 ordered qualifiers, the number 5 qualifier's opening match will be played against the number 12 qualifier.

152. C
Tee markers should be placed 6 yards apart in the teeing area.

153. D

A tournament pairing sheet typically lists the format of the event, handicaps, and tournament officials.

154. B

The competitor's official score is 78.

155. B

The Blind Bogey handicap system matches a competitor's net score to a randomly selected number between 70 and 90.

156. D

The Callaway handicap system deducts a number of the worst hole scores from the combined score of the first 16 holes.

157. C

The three parts of the PGA Teaching Triangle are what, how, and when.

158. D

The three forms of learning the golf swing are verbal, visual, and kinesthetic.

159. False

The four parts of the basic golf swing learning model are input, integration, output, and feedback.

160. True

The three functions of a golf instructor providing feedback to a student are to fix an error, provide motivation, and serve as reinforcement.

161. False

When an instructor and student are developing goals, they should be as specific as possible.

162. B

The "critical error" is a single error the student makes that causes additional errors to be made. The "master key" is to fix the central error because it will help fix other errors as well.

163. B

An inflation adjustment provision provides an annual cost of living increase correlated with the Consumer Price Index (CPI).

164. D
Arbitration can be either voluntary or mandatory, and binding or non-binding. It is less expensive, and less time consuming than litigation.

165. C
Deferred compensation is an arrangement in which a portion of the golf professional's income is paid out at a date after which the income is actually earned. Examples include pensions, retirement plans, and stock options.

166. D
A merger clause found in an employment contract explains what will happen to a golf professional if his or her golf facility is bought or merged with another.

167. C
The key elements found in an employment contract are the term of the contract, the duties and responsibilities of the employer, the duties and responsibilities of the position, compensation, policies on time off, termination clause, and special circumstances.

168. True
Employment contracts may specify that in the event of any controversy or claim arising from the contract, the matter will be subject to arbitration.

169. B
An evergreen clause found in an employment contract provides an automatic annual extension of the contract as long as neither party notifies the other that they wish to terminate the agreement.

170. B
A typical long-term disability insurance policy will pay a disabled employee a maximum benefit of 60% to 66% of his or her pre-disability income.

171. C
Use of employer-provided on-premise athletic facilities is a non-taxable fringe benefit to an employee.

172. True
Free meals and lodging provided to a PGA Professional for the employer's convenience are non-taxable fringe benefits.

173. A

According to the US Department of Labor Child Labor Rules, 14- and 15-year-old minors may work no more than 3 hours on a school day, and 8 hours on a non-school day.

174. D

According to the US Department of Labor Child Labor Rules, 14- and 15-year-old minors may work no more than 18 hours per week when school is in session, and 40 hours per week when school is not in session.

175. False

According to the US Department of Labor Child Labor Rules, 14- and 15-year-old minors may not work before 7:00 am or after 7:00 pm.

176. A

The Fair Labor Standards Act of 1938 established a national minimum wage and set overtime pay requirements.

177. D

The Equal Pay Act of 1963 was passed to amend the Fair Labor Standards Act and make it illegal to pay workers lower wages strictly on the basis on their sex.

178. A

The Occupational Safety and Health Act (OSHA) requires employers to provide employees with a safe and healthy work environment.

179. C

ERISA requires retirement plans to provide participants with important information about plan features and funding.

180. D

The Immigration Reform and Control Act (IRCA) requires employers to verify the identity and work status of each new employee the company hires.

181. True

The Veterans Rights and Military Service Act requires companies to rehire employees who were called to, or volunteered for, military service.

182. False

According to garnishment laws, a court order is required in order to have an employer withhold a specific amount of money from an employee's wage for payment of a debt to a third party. For example, child support, bankruptcy, or unpaid taxes.

183. D
The Age Discrimination in Employment Act (ADEA) prohibits employers from discriminating against workers who are older than age 40.

184. True
The Civil Rights Act states that it is illegal for a company to decide not to hire an applicant for a position because of the applicant's gender, race, or religion.

185. True
The Equal Pay Act requires equal pay for equal work, regardless of sex.

186. False
The Americans with Disabilities Act (ADA) prohibits employers from discriminating against a qualified disabled worker. However, the worker must be able to perform all of the duties required for the job.

187. A
The Fair Labor Standards Act is concerned with record keeping, overtime pay, child labor standards, and minimum wage.

188. A
According to Federal Wage and Hour laws, a golf professional's overtime pay is required to be time and a half.

189. B
Employers who have 20 or more employees are subject to COBRA rules.

190. D
COBRA coverage is limited to 18 months for employees, and 36 months for dependents of employees.

191. False
According to the Fair Credit Reporting Act, if an employer would like to conduct a background check or credit check on an applicant, they must inform the applicant in writing.

192. D
Employment services provided by the PGA include Career Net, Career Links, and Career Chips.

193. A

Career Net is an online job posting service that helps PGA Head Professionals hire assistants and other staff.

194. B

The three basic types of résumés are functional, targeted, and chronological.

195. D

The chronological résumé is most commonly used to apply for job openings in the golf industry.

196. D

Community service, military service, and extracurricular activities should be included on a résumé.

197. B

Professional affiliations should be included on a résumé. Religious and social affiliations should be excluded.

198. A

A golf professional should not specifically ask for a job during a networking call. However, he or she may ask for information about the facility and for names of decision makers.

199. B

In today's golf industry there are more trained golf professionals than golf facilities.

200. False

There are approximately 28,000 men and women PGA Professionals and PGA Apprentices.

LEVEL 2

QUESTIONS

1. **A golf facility's mission statement guides the actions of the facility, describes its goals, and provides a summary of its overall purpose.**

   True
   False

2. **A mission statement should include goals regarding a golf facility's image, quality of service, profitability, and needs of the employer.**

   True
   False

3. **Most golf facilities draw a majority of their clientele from within a _____ mile radius.**

   A. 0 to 5
   B. 5 to 10
   C. 10 to 30
   D. 60 to 90

4. **A SWOT analysis is a strategic business planning tool used to evaluate which of the following?**

   A. Strengths, weaknesses, objectives, threats
   B. Strengths, weaknesses, opportunities, threats
   C. Services, weaknesses, opportunities, techniques
   D. Services, weaknesses, objectives, threats

5. **Which of the following components of a SWOT analysis evaluate external, rather than internal factors of a golf facility?**

    A. Services and weaknesses
    B. Objectives and techniques
    C. Strengths and weaknesses
    D. Opportunities and threats

6. **Which of the following formulas is used to conduct a linear trend analysis?**

    A. (previous year sales – later year sales) / previous year sales = % change
    B. (later year sales – previous year sales) x previous year sales = % change
    C. (later year sales – previous year sales) x later year sales = % change
    D. (later year sales – previous year sales) / previous year sales = % change

7. **The Golf Shop had sales over the past three years of $55,000 (2009), $60,000 (2010), and $70,000 (2011). Using linear trend analysis, what are the projected total sales for next year?**

    A. $77,384
    B. $78,210
    C. $79,016
    D. $80,233

8. **Which of the following formulas is used to conduct a base-year analysis?**

    A. (year's sales you want to compare / base year sales) x 100 = % change from base year
    B. (base year sales / year's sales you want to compare) x 100 = % change from base year
    C. (year's sales to want to compare / base year sales) / 100 = % change from base year
    D. (base year sales / year's sales you want to compare) / 100 = % change from base year

9. The Golf Shop had sales over the past three years of $55,000 (2009), $60,000 (2010), and $70,000 (2011). Using base-year analysis with 2009 as the base year, what is the index number for 2011?

A. 1.27
B. 1.36
C. 1.45
D. 1.54

10. The Golf Shop had sales over the past three years of $55,000 (2009), $60,000 (2010), and $70,000 (2011). Using base-year analysis with 2010 as the base year, what is the index number for 2011?

A. 1.05
B. 1.17
C. 1.22
D. 1.43

11. Which type of analysis should be used if a Head Professional intends to track improved golf shop sales relative to the year he was hired?

A. Linear trend analysis
B. Base-year analysis

12. Which type of analysis should be used to calculate the percentage change from year to year for line items such as rounds played, revenues, and expenses?

A. Linear trend analysis
B. Base-year analysis

13. Linear trend analysis is recommended when there is over _____ years of historical data to compare, and the data is being compared _____ over those years.

A. 5, Vertically
B. 2, Horizontally
C. 2, Vertically
D. 5, Horizontally

14. All but which of the following are types of budgets?

A. Cash flow budget
B. Operational budget
C. Income budget
D. Capital budget

15. Which of the following is the first step of the budgeting process?

A. List all categories and amounts of fixed expenses.
B. Determine how much needs to be saved.
C. Estimate all income and sources of income.
D. List all categories and amounts of discretionary expenses.

16. Which type of budget projects how much cash a golf facility should have in its bank account at the end of each budget period?

A. Cash flow budget
B. Operational budget
C. Income budget
D. Capital budget

17. Which type of budget includes the cost of financing long-term projects, such as renovations to the golf course and its buildings?

A. Cash flow budget
B. Operational budget
C. Income budget
D. Capital budget

18. Which type of budget provides an overview of the golf facility's day-to-day income and expenses? It is a short-term budget that does not include long-term projects.

A. Cash flow budget
B. Operational budget
C. Income budget
D. Capital budget

19. Which of the following formulas is used to calculate profit?

    A. Profit = (expenses − cost of goods sold) − revenue
    B. Profit = (cost of goods sold + expenses) − revenue
    C. Profit = revenue − (cost of goods sold − expenses)
    D. Profit = revenue − (cost of goods sold + expenses)

20. Last year, The Golf Shop had revenues of $80,000. Of that amount, the cost of goods sold was $35,000, and other miscellaneous expenses totaled $25,000. What was the annual profit?

    A. $20,000
    B. $35,000
    C. $45,000
    D. $55,000

21. If The Golf Shop had annual revenues of $60,000, cost of goods sold of $20,000, and a $30,000 profit, how much were the miscellaneous expenses for the year?

    A. $10,000
    B. $20,000
    C. $30,000
    D. $40,000

22. Which of the following formulas is used to calculate gross margin %?

    A. Gross margin % = (revenue − cost of goods sold) / revenue
    B. Gross margin % = (cost of goods sold − revenue) / revenue
    C. Gross margin % = (revenue − cost of goods sold) / cost of goods sold
    D. Gross margin % = (cost of goods sold − revenue) / cost of goods sold

23. The Golf Shop's Q1 revenue was $46,745. Of that amount, $29,540 was attributed to cost of goods sold. Calculate the gross margin %.

    A. 24.4%
    B. 36.8%
    C. 48.1%
    D. None of the above

24. If The Golf Shop had annual revenues of $120,000, and a gross margin percentage of 18.5%, what were the cost of goods sold for the year?

A. $92,600
B. $96,200
C. $97,800
D. None of the above

25. Which of the following formulas is used to calculate cost of goods sold (COGS) %?

A. COGS % = cost of goods sold x total retail sales
B. COGS % = cost of goods sold / total retail sales
C. COGS % = total retail sales / cost of goods sold
D. COGS % = cost of goods sold − total retail sales

26. Last year, The Golf Shop had retail sales of $122,380. Of that amount, $101,200 was attributed to cost of goods sold. Calculate the COGS %.

A. 17.3%
B. 20.9%
C. 82.7%
D. 85.1%

27. Last year, The Golf Shop had annual retail sales of $99,300 and a margin of $28,750. Calculate the COGS %.

A. 56.95%
B. 61.20%
C. 66.35%
D. 71.05%

28. If The Golf Shop had a COGS % of 75% and annual retail sales of $90,000, what was their margin?

A. $22,500
B. $67,500
C. $90,000
D. None of the above

29. **Which of the following formulas is used to calculate the net total value of a depreciable asset?**

    A. Net total value = original cost – accumulated depreciation
    B. Net total value = original cost + accumulated depreciation
    C. Net total value = accumulated depreciation – original cost
    D. Net total value = accumulated depreciation / original cost

30. **Calculate the net total value of a piece of machinery with an initial cost of $35,000, and accumulated depreciation of $12,400.**

    A. $12,400
    B. $22,600
    C. $24,800
    D. $35,000

31. **Which of the following describes the process by which the tax basis of a tangible asset is recovered?**

    A. Amortization
    B. Depreciation
    C. Depletion
    D. All of the above

32. **Which of the following describes the process by which the tax basis of an intangible asset is recovered?**

    A. Amortization
    B. Depreciation
    C. Depletion
    D. All of the above

33. Which of the following describes the process by which the tax basis of natural resources is recovered?

A. Amortization
B. Depreciation
C. Depletion
D. All of the above

34. All but which of the following are internal factors that affect a golf facility's economic forecast?

A. Staff resources
B. Golf industry trends
C. Facility characteristics
D. Financial resources

35. All but which of the following are external factors that affect a golf facility's economic forecast?

A. Customer services
B. National economic trends
C. The weather
D. Golf industry trends

36. All but which of the following are aspects of effective staffing?

A. Establish clear performance standards
B. Determine staff needs and skills
C. Use organizational charts to clarify reporting relationships
D. All of the above are aspects of effective staffing.

37. Which of the following is/are correct regarding a golf facility's policies and procedures?

   (1) Procedures are rules or principles provided by management that outline a definite course of action.
   (2) Policies are step-by-step instructions which must be executed in a certain manner to complete a specific task.

   A. (1) only
   B. (2) only
   C. All of the above
   D. None of the above

38. Any experience customers have with a business that provides them with an opportunity to evaluate the quality of their products and services is referred to as a _____.

   A. Selling point
   B. Moment of clarity
   C. Moment of truth
   D. Turning point

39. When guests arrive at a golf club to find dirty towels lying in the locker room, they are experiencing a "moment of truth".

   True
   False

40. When golfers encounter a frost delay during the morning of a tournament, they are experiencing a "moment of truth".

   True
   False

41. Which of the following are among the key elements to achieving successful customer service?

    A. Staffing
    B. Systems
    C. Resources
    D. All of the above

42. It is estimated that 50% of dissatisfied customers do not complain directly.

    True
    False

43. What percentage of dissatisfied customers will not return to a golf facility?

    A. 25%
    B. 50%
    C. 75%
    D. 90%

44. It is estimated that one unhappy customer will tell how many others?

    A. 1
    B. 2
    C. 5
    D. 9

45. Approximately 13% of dissatisfied customers will tell at least 20 people.

    True
    False

46. Which of the following are key questions a golf professional should ask himself according to the Task-Relation Connection?

(1) "How does the way I handle this task build or detract from the relationship?"
(2) "How does the way I handle the relationship with the other person support or limit finishing the task?"

A. (1) only
B. (2) only
C. All of the above
D. None of the above

47. All but which of the following are part of the **GEODE** model for handling day-to-day customer relations?

A. Enquire
B. Give
C. Offer
D. Deliver

48. All but which of the following are part of the **GEODE** model for handling day-to-day customer relations?

A. Evaluate
B. Deliver
C. Empathy
D. Offer

49. According to the **GEODE** model, in which step should the golf professional show understanding and empathy?

A. Deliver
B. Enquire
C. Offer
D. Evaluate

50. According to the **GEODE** model, in which step should the golf professional propose a solution and describe limitations sympathetically?

A. Greet
B. Enquire
C. Deliver
D. Offer

51. According to the **GEODE** model, in which step should the golf professional determine specific arrangements and provide a meaningful extra touch?

A. Evaluate
B. Deliver
C. Offer
D. Enquire

52. During which step of the **GEODE** model should the golf professional confirm the customer's need by restating the customer's concerns and checking for agreement?

A. Greet
B. Enquire
C. Deliver
D. Offer

53. During which step of the **GEODE** model should the golf professional frame the customer interaction as problem-solving rather than confrontational?

A. Enquire
B. Offer
C. Greet
D. Evaluate

54. **Which interpersonal skill bridges the gap between what the golf professional offers and what the customer wants?**

    A. Showing understanding
    B. Reframing difficult situations
    C. Acting with integrity
    D. Providing a compelling rationale

55. **Which interpersonal skill establishes direction and alignment?**

    A. Stating your purpose clearly
    B. Encouraging open expression
    C. Inviting and giving specific feedback
    D. Acting with integrity

56. **Which interpersonal skill evokes participation through active involvement?**

    A. Inviting and giving specific feedback
    B. Encouraging open expression
    C. Acting with integrity
    D. Reframing difficult situations

57. **Which interpersonal skill reduces defensiveness by establishing empathy?**

    A. Reframing difficult situations
    B. Providing a compelling rationale
    C. Inviting and giving specific feedback
    D. Showing understanding

58. **Which interpersonal skill finds positive intent that may be hidden in a negative response?**

    A. Reframing difficult situations
    B. Showing understanding
    C. Stating your purpose clearly
    D. Inviting and giving specific feedback

59.Which interpersonal skill allows the golf professional to be assertive without being overbearing through the use of "I" statements?

A. Encouraging open expression
B. Stating your purpose clearly
C. Acting with integrity
D. Providing a compelling rationale

60.The interpersonal skill "encouraging open expression" suggests the golf professional should establish a receptive and nonjudgmental stance with the customer.

True
False

61.The interpersonal skill "acting with integrity" recommends the use of analogies as a technique to introduce a fresh perspective.

True
False

62.Which interaction strategy helps others see the value of adopting your solution?

A. Directing
B. Convincing
C. Involving
D. Supporting

63.Which interaction strategy helps others find their own problem solving solution?

A. Directing
B. Convincing
C. Involving
D. Supporting

64. **Which interaction strategy invites others to join with your solution?**

A. Directing
B. Convincing
C. Involving
D. Supporting

65. **Which interaction strategy involves telling others explicitly what to do?**

A. Directing
B. Convincing
C. Involving
D. Supporting

66. **Which interaction strategy should a Superintendent use when explaining the safety rules of a new and potentially dangerous piece of equipment?**

A. Directing
B. Convincing
C. Involving
D. Supporting

67. **The "directing" strategy should be used to help two friends solve a disagreement.**

True
False

68. **Which interaction strategy is being used if a golf professional lists several reasons why the current practice facilities should be expanded, and then presents the reasons to the Board of Directors?**

A. Directing
B. Convincing
C. Involving
D. Supporting

69. When explaining membership benefits to a potential new golf club member, the golf professional should use the "directing" strategy.

   True
   False

70. The factors that make an exceptional golf instructor are communication skills, motivation, energy, enthusiasm, golf knowledge, and credibility.

   True
   False

71. "Trade outs", or offering green fees or lessons to a radio, newspaper, or television station for payment of a golf facility's commercial message is unethical and should be avoided.

   True
   False

72. If a PGA Professional charges $50 per hour for individual lessons, or $35 per person for group lessons of 2 to 4 students, how much potential revenue will be lost if 4 students sign up for a group lesson? Assume the 4 students would have otherwise signed up for individual lessons.

   A. $60
   B. $140
   C. $200
   D. $250

73. According to PGA Professional Craig Shankland, the maximum number of lessons an instructor should teach per day should not exceed 10 half-hour lessons, or 6 one-hour lessons.

   True
   False

74. All but which of the following are key elements used to evaluate whether a golf club will improve a player's performance?

A. Quality
B. Quantity available
C. Design
D. Fit

75. The flex characteristics of graphite shafts are controlled primarily by wall thickness.

True
False

76. Graphite shafts transmit _____ vibrations up the shaft to a golfer's hands than steel shafts.

A. More
B. Fewer

77. The thinner the shaft, the _____ torque it will have.

A. More
B. Less

78. The thicker the shaft, the _____ and _____ it will be.

A. Less stiff, Lighter
B. Stiffer, Heavier
C. Stiffer, Lighter
D. Less stiff, Heavier

79. The stiffness, flex points, and torque of _____ shafts are controlled by the fiber's tensile strength, the amount of fiber, and the pattern in which the fibers are applied.

A. Steel
B. Graphite

80. To be legal for events played under **USGA** and **R&A** rules, all golf balls must pass a test on initial velocity, weight, size, symmetry of design pattern, and overall distance.

True
False

81. The distance a golf ball travels is affected by its size, weight, and dimple design, but is not affected by the material of its cover and core.

True
False

82. Golf ball performance is distinguished by compression, durability, and material, but not by aerodynamics. This is because aerodynamics is a law that does not change among golf balls.

True
False

83. For iron shots, the clubhead should strike the ball with a/an _____ arc.

A. Ascending
B. Descending
C. Level

84. For iron shots, the clubhead's center of gravity at impact should be equal to, or _____ than, that of the center of gravity of the ball.

A. Higher
B. Lower

85. The golf course Superintendent is entrusted with the maintenance, operation, and management of a golf course.

True
False

86. The golf course Superintendent must achieve and document compliance with all but which of the following regulatory agencies?

A. EPA
B. ADEA
C. OSHA
D. All of the above

87. The basic zones of turfgrass adaptation in the United States are cool season grass, warm season grass, and temperate season grass.

True
False

88. How many basic zones of turfgrass adaptation are present in the United States?

A. 2
B. 3
C. 5
D. 6

89. All but which of the following are northern climate grasses?

A. Bermudagrass
B. Bluegrass
C. Ryegrass
D. Fescues

90. All but which of the following are southern climate grasses?

A. Zoysiagrass
B. Buffalograss
C. Bentgrass
D. Bermudagrass

91. Cool season grasses thrive in temperatures ranging from _____ degrees.

A. 30 to 45
B. 45 to 60
C. 60 to 75
D. 75 to 90

92. In areas that receive snow, how are cool season grasses affected?

A. They continue to grow and stay green.
B. They become dormant and turn brown.
C. They become dormant but stay green.
D. They continue to grow but turn brown.

93. Warm season grasses thrive in temperatures ranging from _____ degrees.

A. 50 to 65
B. 65 to 80
C. 80 to 95
D. 95 to 110

94. There are _____ essential nutrients for turfgrass that occur naturally in sufficient quantities in the air. _____ essential nutrients may be supplemented through fertilizers.

    A. 8, 8
    B. 12, 4
    C. 15, 3
    D. 16, 6

95. Which of the following is/are correct regarding the growing points of plants and grass?

    (1) In plants, the growing point is at the tip of the shoot.
    (2) In grass, the growing point is at the base of the shoot.

    A. (1) only
    B. (2) only
    C. All of the above
    D. None of the above

96. Which of the following is/are correct regarding the shoots and roots of a plant?

    (1) Shoots need sunlight in order to absorb water and nutrients.
    (2) Roots produce food for the plant.

    A. (1) only
    B. (2) only
    C. All of the above
    D. None of the above

97. Sandy soil allows water to pass through quickly, while loam soil tends to retain water.

    True
    False

98. Soil can be classified by the _____ of its particles.

A. Color
B. Size
C. Density
D. Temperature

99. Which type of soil creates a stable growing environment for a plant by providing the best balance between drainage and retention?

A. Clay soil
B. Loam soil
C. Sandy soil
D. None of the above

100. Which type of soil is composed of large particles that allow water and nutrients to pass through so quickly that they are not readily available for the plant?

A. Clay soil
B. Loam soil
C. Sandy soil
D. None of the above

101. Soil pH measures soil acidity and alkalinity.

True
False

102. On the soil pH scale, a measure of 0 is highly _____, and a measure of 14 is highly _____.

A. Acidic, Neutral
B. Alkaline, Neutral
C. Acidic, Alkaline
D. Alkaline, Acidic

103. Turfgrass grows best in soils that are _____.

    A. Slightly acidic
    B. Slightly alkaline
    C. Neutral
    D. Highly acidic

104. Clay soil tends to be acidic.

    True
    False

105. Sandy soil tends to be acidic.

    True
    False

106. Which of the following may be added to soil to raise its pH level?

    A. Lime
    B. Sulfur
    C. Phosphorus
    D. Calcium

107. Which of the following may be added to soil to lower its pH level?

    A. Lime
    B. Sulfur
    C. Phosphorus
    D. Calcium

108. A technique called _____ may be used to cool off turfgrass through a light application of water to the grass surface.

    A. Irrigating
    B. Draining
    C. Syringing
    D. Infusing

109. When should syringing be applied to turfgrass?

    A. During healthy growing cycles
    B. At the first sign of wilt
    C. Immediately following rainfall
    D. None of the above

110. During excessive heat, syringing may be applied up to _____ times daily.

    A. 3
    B. 5
    C. 10
    D. 12

111. Grasses that best tolerate shorter mowing heights are bluegrass and ryegrass.

    True
    False

112. Shorter grass tends to be healthier than longer grass.

    True
    False

113. **Ryegrass is commonly used as rough on a golf course because of its low maintenance requirements.**

    True
    False

114. **Removing the shoot reduces a plant's resistance to the invasion of disease.**

    True
    False

115. **Removing the shoot increases a plant's ability to absorb water and nutrients.**

    True
    False

116. **Removing the shoot increases a plant's ability to make its own food.**

    True
    False

117. **Grasses are able to regenerate their shoots if they are not cut too closely to their growing points.**

    True
    False

118. **Which of the following is the suggested mowing height for greens?**

    A. 1/32" to 1/16"
    B. 1/16" to 1/8"
    C. 1/8" to 1/4"
    D. 1/4" to 1/2"

119.Which of the following is the suggested mowing height for tees?

    A. 1/16" to 1/8"
    B. 3/8" to 1"
    C. 3/4" to 1"
    D. 1" to 1¼"

120.Which of the following is the suggested mowing height for fairways?

    A. 1/4" to 1/2"
    B. 1/2" to 1¼"
    C. 3/4" to 1"
    D. 1" to 1¼"

121.Which of the following is the suggested mowing height for rough?

    A. 1" or higher
    B. 2" or higher
    C. 3" or higher
    D. 4" or higher

122. Longer mowing heights create a turfgrass environment that requires more active maintenance.

    True
    False

123.Tees and fairways should be mowed 2 to 4 times per week depending on golf course conditions.

    True
    False

124. Greens should never be mowed more than once per day.

True
False

125. A bag of fertilizer that reads 10-6-4 will contain 10% _____, 6% _____, and 4% _____.

A. Nitrogen, Potassium, Phosphorus
B. Potassium, Nitrogen, Phosphorus
C. Potassium, Phosphorus, Nitrogen
D. Nitrogen, Phosphorus, Potassium

126. Soils are approximately _____ air, _____ water, and _____ solid.

A. 25%, 25%, 50%
B. 10%, 40%, 50%
C. 33%, 33%, 34%
D. 5%, 5%, 90%

127. Aeration involves removing 3 to 4 inches of soil from the ground.

True
False

128. Aeration stimulates the growth of new roots by decreasing the air supply to the roots and not allowing water and nutrients to penetrate into the root zone.

True
False

129. Aeration removes the passageways in soil that facilitate the flow of water, nutrients, and air to the plant.

True
False

130. **Excess thatch prevents water, nutrients, fertilizers, and pesticides from penetrating into the soil and plant roots.**

    True
    False

131. **Which of the following is the practice of placing a layer of soil over the putting surface to smooth and decrease surface irregularity?**

    A. Thatching
    B. Topdressing
    C. Topseeding
    D. Overseeding

132. **Aeration is often performed immediately after topdressing in order to create holes for the topdressing to reach the plant roots.**

    True
    False

133. **Overseeding is used primarily in which areas of the country?**

    A. Northern
    B. Southern
    C. Eastern
    D. Western

134. **Overseeding involves planting _____ season grasses over _____ season grasses.**

    A. Cool, Warm
    B. Warm, Cool
    C. Warm, Warm
    D. Cool, Cool

135. **For insect prevention on turfgrass, thatch should be kept at a minimum.**

    True
    False

136. **The three broad categories of pests found on golf courses are insects, animals, and diseases.**

    True
    False

137. **A weed is simply defined as a plant in an undesired location.**

    True
    False

138. **Which of the following should be used to kill unwanted plants on a golf course?**

    A. Fungicide
    B. Herbicide
    C. Insecticide
    D. Pesticide

139. **Segregated Pest Control (SPC) places an emphasis on prevention, rather than eradication. According to SPC, the Superintendent should take appropriate, but minimum action at first, and only take additional action if necessary.**

    True
    False

140. **Thick thatch allows essential nutrients and insecticides to reach the turfgrass, increasing its overall health.**

    True
    False

141. **Which of the following occurs when the weight of heavy machinery compresses soil and causes a loss of pore space?**

   A. Soil degradation
   B. Soil impaction
   C. Soil compaction
   D. Soil contraction

142. **Plants are classified by their lifecycle and plant structure.**

   True
   False

143. **All but which of the following are common surface insects found on a golf course?**

   A. Armyworms
   B. Sod webworms
   C. Vegetable weevils
   D. White grubs

144. **All but which of the following are common subsurface insects found on a golf course?**

   A. Bermudagrass mites
   B. Chinch bugs
   C. Centipedes
   D. Nematodes

145. **Overall thinning of turf is a warning sign that subsurface insects may be present.**

   True
   False

146. Turf that is beginning to die along curbs or sidewalks, even with adequate watering, is an indication of which of the following?

A. Surface insects are present.
B. Subsurface insects are present.
C. Either surface or subsurface insects are present.
D. A turf problem other than insects exists.

147. Turfgrass disease is primarily a result of which of the following?

A. Insects
B. Fungi
C. Weeds
D. Drought

148. Which of the following is a layer of organic matter that accumulates just below the grass blades and above the soil surface? It may be harmful and should be removed.

A. Fungi
B. Mildew
C. Soil
D. Thatch

149. All but which of the following are common turfgrass diseases found on a golf course?

A. Brown patch
B. Poa pratensis
C. Dollar spot
D. All of the above are common turfgrass diseases.

150. All but which of the following are common turfgrass diseases found on a golf course?

A. Fairy ring
B. Grease spot
C. Dollar spot
D. All of the above are common turfgrass diseases.

151. The Head Professional is responsible for overseeing a turfgrass management program that provides a playing surface that meets the golf club's aesthetic and playing standards, while at the same time preserving the natural environment.

True
False

152. The Superintendent's responsibilities include managing the golf course, grounds surrounding the golf course, practice putting greens, golf range, parking lot, and entrance road.

True
False

153. Which of the following individuals is responsible for hiring, training, evaluating, and managing the year-round and seasonal maintenance staff?

A. Head Professional
B. Director of Golf
C. Superintendent
D. General Manager

154. All but which of the following phases of golf course design are paired with the correct description?

A. Phase V: Maintenance
B. Phase II: Design
C. Phase IV: Grow-in
D. Phase I: Development

155. All but which of the following phases of golf course design are paired with the correct description?

A. Phase II: Site analysis
B. Phase IV: Grow-in
C. Phase V: Maintenance
D. Phase III: Development

156. The site analysis phase of the golf course design process takes approximately
_____ months to complete.

    A. 3 to 10
    B. 4 to 6
    C. 6 to 18
    D. 12 to 18

157. The design phase of the golf course design process takes approximately _____
months to complete.

    A. 3 to 10
    B. 4 to 6
    C. 6 to 18
    D. 12 to 18

158. The development phase of the golf course design process takes approximately
_____ months to complete.

    A. 3 to 10
    B. 4 to 6
    C. 6 to 18
    D. 12 to 18

159. The grow-in phase of the golf course design process takes approximately
_____ months to complete.

    A. 3 to 10
    B. 4 to 6
    C. 6 to 18
    D. 12 to 18

160. In Phase II of the golf course design process, the proper steps placed in the correct order are:

    A. Base map, routing plan, construction plan, concept plan
    B. Concept plan, base map, routing Plan, construction plan
    C. Base map, routing plan, concept plan, construction plan
    D. Concept plan, construction plan, routing plan, base map

161. The _____, as part of the golf course design process, should include underground utilities, right-of-ways, structures, historical sites, and environmental resources such as wetlands.

    A. Base map
    B. Construction plan
    C. Concept plan
    D. Routing plan

162. The routing plan, as part of the golf course design process, may also be referred to as a schematic.

    True
    False

163. The first step to developing a routing plan is to identify which of the following?

    A. Possible locations for the 1st tee
    B. Possible locations for the practice facility
    C. Possible locations for the clubhouse
    D. Possible locations for the parking lot

164. Which of the following provides a visual image of how a golf course will look once it is complete?

    A. Routing plan
    B. Base map
    C. Construction plan
    D. Concept plan

165. Which of the following displays the shape, size, and form of each golf course feature, including tees, greens, bunkers, and hazards?

   A. Routing plan
   B. Base map
   C. Construction plan
   D. Concept plan

166. Which of the following is a detailed drawing used to guide the building of a golf course? It includes specific plans for irrigation, landscaping, grading, and other course features.

   A. Construction plan
   B. Concept plan
   C. Base plan
   D. Routing plan

167. Which of the following marks the end of the golf course design phase, and provides the basis for the development phase?

   A. Finalizing the routing plan
   B. Finalizing the base map
   C. Finalizing the construction plan
   D. Finalizing the concept plan

168. The development phase of the golf course design process includes seven steps in the following order: staking, clearing, rough grading and major drainage, feature construction and minor drainage, irrigation, finished grading and planting preparation, and planting.

   True
   False

169. **Major earth moving occurs during which step of the golf course development phase?**

   A. Clearing
   B. Rough grading and major drainage
   C. Feature construction and minor drainage
   D. Finished grading and planting preparation

170. **Small bulldozers shape the final form of the golf course as part of which step of the golf course development phase?**

   A. Clearing
   B. Rough grading and major drainage
   C. Feature construction and minor drainage
   D. Finished grading and planting preparation

171. **Golf course irrigation systems may be automatic or manual, single line or double line, electric or hydraulic.**

   True
   False

172. **When planting a newly developed golf course, the rough should be planted first, then fairways, and finally tees and greens.**

   True
   False

173. **The grow-in period of golf course design often takes over two years to complete.**

   True
   False

174. All but which of the following are members of the core team responsible for designing and developing a golf course?

   A. Architect
   B. Irrigation specialist
   C. Superintendent
   D. Contractor

175. The contractor is typically hired at the end of the golf course _____ phase through a bidding process.

   A. Site analysis
   B. Development
   C. Grow-in
   D. Design

176. The Superintendent assumes the lead at the end of the _____ phase, and consults with the architect as needed.

   A. Site analysis
   B. Development
   C. Grow-in
   D. Design

177. The Head Professional works most closely with which of the following individuals during the golf course design process?

   A. Contractor
   B. Superintendent
   C. Architect
   D. Irrigation specialist

178. Land planners, environmentalists, hydrologists, archaeologists, legal counsel, and financial advisors are employed during the _____ phase of the golf course design process.

A. Design
B. Development
C. Site analysis
D. Grow-in

179. Interior designers, publicists, landscape architects, and building architects are employed during the _____ phase of the golf course design process.

A. Design
B. Development
C. Site analysis
D. Grow-in

180. Bricklayers, concrete pourers, irrigation specialists, and heavy equipment operators are employed during the _____ phase of the golf course design process.

A. Design
B. Grow-in
C. Maintenance
D. Development

181. Surface drainage is the slope and shape of the land.

True
False

182. Subsurface drainage is the internal drainage of the soil.

True
False

183. Surface drainage is primarily a function of soil content.

True
False

184. Subsurface drainage is primarily a function of the land's topography.

True
False

185. Subsurface drainage systems are typically used in areas of a golf course that require the least maintenance, such as rough areas.

True
False

186. Which of the following methods are used to create adequate subsurface drainage?

A. Soil amendments
B. Construction of drainage systems
C. Soil amendments and construction of drainage systems
D. None of the above

187. When constructing greens, use layered soils with a combination of coarse and fine textures to produce a balance between retention and drainage.

True
False

188. All but which of the following are modern methods of constructing greens?

A. California Greens Construction Method
B. Florida Greens Construction Method
C. Topsoil Greens Construction Method
D. USGA Greens Construction Method

189. The tee area for each hole should be at least _____ square feet, which is large enough to allow for frequent movement of tee markers.

   A. 500
   B. 2,000
   C. 6,000
   D. 10,000

190. Because they receive more wear, the first, tenth, and par-3 tees usually average _____ square feet or more.

   A. 8,000
   B. 10,000
   C. 12,000
   D. 14,000

191. Greens sizes typically range from _____ square feet at a **PGA** recognized golf course.

   A. 1,000 to 4,000
   B. 5,000 to 8,000
   C. 10,000 to 12,000
   D. 15,000 to 20,000

192. There should be a _____ foot collar around the perimeter of each green where no cups should be placed.

   A. 3 to 5
   B. 5 to 7
   C. 12 to 15
   D. 15 to 20

193. A green should have 12 to 20 areas for possible cup placement, with a _____ foot radius around the cup with no slope.

   A. 1
   B. 3
   C. 4
   D. 5

194. The landing area following a tee shot should be at least 200 to 250 square feet at a minimum.

   True
   False

195. Adjacent tees and greens should be 200 feet apart at their borders, and 400 feet apart from their center points.

   True
   False

196. Golf holes should be routed _____ to allow right-handed golfers to _____ into the course, not out of bounds.

   A. Clockwise, Slice
   B. Clockwise, Hook
   C. Counterclockwise, Slice
   D. Counterclockwise, Hook

197. The recreational golf experience is divided into five phases: anticipation, arrival, participation, cool down, and memory.

   True
   False

198. Which of the following is/are correct regarding golf hole design?

    (1) A penal golf hole design is not forgiving because it leaves little room for error.
    (2) A strategic golf hole requires extraordinary maneuvers.

    A. (1) only
    B. (2) only
    C. All of the above
    D. None of the above

199. Which of the following is/are correct regarding the contour of the tee area?

    (1) The golfer should be able to view the entire hole from the tee-off position.
    (2) The contour of the tee area should not necessarily direct the golfer towards the intended line of play.

    A. (1) only
    B. (2) only
    C. All of the above
    D. None of the above

200. Hazards should not be used to direct play, but should instead provide depth perception, variety, and challenge.

    True
    False

ANSWER KEY

1. True
A golf facility's mission statement guides the actions of the facility, describes its goals, and provides a summary of its overall purpose.

2. False
A mission statement should include goals regarding a golf facility's image, quality of service, profitability, and employee needs.

3. C
Most golf facilities draw a majority of their clientele from within a 10 to 30 mile radius.

4. B
A SWOT analysis is a strategic business planning tool used to evaluate a company's strengths, weaknesses, opportunities, and threats.

5. D
Opportunities and threats evaluate external, rather than internal factors of a golf facility.

6. D
The formula used to conduct a linear trend analysis is:
(later year sales − previous year sales) / previous year sales = % change

7. C
Step 1: ($60,000 - $55,000) / $55,000 = 0.0909
Step 2: ($70,000 - $60,000) / $60,000 = 0.1667
Step 3: 0.0909 + 0.1667 = 0.2576
Step 4: 0.2576 / 2 = 0.1288
Step 5: $70,000 x 1.1288 = $79,016

8. A
The formula used to conduct a base-year analysis is:
(year's sales you want to compare / base year sales) x 100 = % change from base year

9. A
($70,000 / $55,000) = 1.27

10. B
($70,000 / $60,000) = 1.17

11. B
A base-year analysis should be used if a Head Professional intends to track improved golf shop sales relative to the year he was hired.

12. A
A linear trend analysis should be used to calculate the percentage change from year to year for line items such as rounds played, revenues, and expenses.

13. D
Linear trend analysis is recommended when there is over 5 years of historical data to compare, and the data is being compared horizontally over those years.

14. C
The three types of budgets are cash flow, operational, and capital.

15. C
The first step of the budgeting process is to estimate all income and sources of income. The next step is to review all fixed and discretionary expenses before determining how much will be saved or invested.

16. A
A cash flow budget projects how much cash a golf facility should have in its bank account at the end of each budget period.

17. D
A capital budget includes the cost of financing long-term projects, such as renovations to the golf course and its buildings.

18. B
An operational budget provides an overview of the golf facility's day-to-day income and expenses. It is a short-term budget that does not include long-term projects.

19. D
Profit = revenue − (cost of goods sold + expenses)

20. A
Profit = $80,000 − ($35,000 + $25,000)
Profit = $80,000 − $60,000
Profit = $20,000

21. A
$30,000 = $60,000 − ($20,000 + expenses)
Expenses = $10,000

22. A
Gross margin % = (revenue − cost of goods sold) / revenue

23. B
Gross margin % = ($46,745 − $29,540) / $46,745
Gross margin % = $17,205 / $46,745
Gross margin % = 36.8%

24. C
$120,000 x 18.5% = $22,200
$120,000 - $22,200 = $97,800

25. B
COGS % = cost of goods sold / total retail sales

26. C
COGS % = $101,200 / $122,380
COGS % = 82.7%

27. D
$28,750 / $99,300 = 0.2895
1 − 0.2895 = 0.7105 = 71.05%

28. A
$90,000 x 75% = $67,500
$90,000 − $67,500 = $22,500

29. A
Net total value = original cost − accumulated depreciation

30. B
Net total value = $35,000 − $12,400
Net total value = $22,600

31. B
Depreciation is the process by which the tax basis of a tangible asset is recovered.

32. A
Amortization is the process by which the tax basis of an intangible asset is recovered.

33. C
Depletion is the process by which the tax basis of natural resources is recovered.

34. B
Internal factors that affect a golf facility's economic forecast include staff resources, facility characteristics, financial resources, and customer services.

35. A
External factors that affect a golf facility's economic forecast include national economic trends, the weather, golf industry trends, and regulatory trends.

36. D
Aspects of effective staffing include establishing clear performance standards, determining staff needs and skills, and using organizational charts to clarify reporting relationships.

37. D
Policies are rules or principles provided by management that outline a definite course of action. Procedures are step-by-step instructions which must be executed in a certain manner to complete a specific task.

38. C
Any experience customers have with a business that provides them with an opportunity to evaluate the quality of their products and services is referred to as a "moment of truth".

39. True
When guests arrive at a golf club to find dirty towels lying in the locker room, they are experiencing a "moment of truth".

40. False
Frost and weather delays do not directly provide an opportunity for customers to evaluate the quality of a golf club's products and services. Therefore, a weather delay is not a "moment of truth".

41. D

The key elements to achieving successful customer service are staffing, systems, and resources.

42. False

It is estimated that 96% of dissatisfied customers do not complain directly.

43. D

90% of dissatisfied customers will not return to a golf facility.

44. D

One unhappy customer will tell nine others.

45. True

Approximately 13% of dissatisfied customers will tell at least 20 people.

46. C

The key questions a golf professional should ask himself according to the Task-Relation Connection are: "How does the way I handle this task build or detract from the relationship?" and, "How does the way I handle the relationship with the other person support or limit finishing the task?"

47. B

The GEODE model for handling day-to-day customer relations stands for Greet, Enquire, Offer, Deliver, and Evaluate.

48. C

The GEODE model for handling day-to-day customer relations stands for Greet, Enquire, Offer, Deliver, and Evaluate.

49. B

The golf professional shows understanding and empathy during the Enquire step of the GEODE model.

50. D

The golf professional proposes a solution and describes limitations sympathetically during the Offer step of the GEODE model.

51. B

The golf professional determines specific arrangements and provides a meaningful extra touch during the Deliver step of the GEODE model.

52. B
The golf professional confirms the customer's needs by restating the customer's concerns and checking for agreement during the Enquire step of the GEODO model.

53. C
The golf professional frames the customer interaction as problem-solving rather than confrontational during the Greet step of the GEODE model.

54. D
The interpersonal skill "providing a compelling rationale" bridges the gap between what the golf professional offers and what the customer wants.

55. A
The interpersonal skill "stating your purpose clearly" establishes direction and alignment.

56. B
The interpersonal skill "encouraging open expression" evokes participation through active involvement.

57. D
The interpersonal skill "showing understanding" reduces defensiveness by establishing empathy.

58. A
The interpersonal skill "reframing difficult situations" finds positive intent that may be hidden in a negative response.

59. B
The interpersonal skill "stating your purpose clearly" allows the golf professional to be assertive without being overbearing through the use of "I" statements.

60. True
The interpersonal skill "encouraging open expression" suggests the golf professional should establish a receptive and nonjudgmental stance with the customer.

61. False
The interpersonal skill "reframing difficult situations" recommends the use of analogies as a technique to introduce a fresh perspective.

62. B
"Convincing" helps others see the value of adopting your solution.

63. D

"Supporting" helps others find their own problem solving solution.

64. C

"Involving" invites others to join with your solution.

65. A

"Directing" involves telling others explicitly what to do.

66. A

A Superintendent should use the "directing" strategy when explaining the safety rules of a new and potentially dangerous piece of equipment.

67. False

The "involving" strategy should be used to help two friends solve a disagreement.

68. B

A golf professional is using the "convincing" strategy if he lists several reasons why the current practice facilities should be expanded, and then presents the reasons to the Board of Directors.

69. False

The golf professional should use the "convincing" strategy when explaining membership benefits to a potential new golf club member.

70. True

The factors that make an exceptional golf instructor are communication skills, motivation, energy, enthusiasm, golf knowledge, and credibility.

71. False

Trade outs are an appropriate method for advertising and promoting golf services.

72. A

Individual rate: 4 students x $50 = $200
Group rate: 4 students x $35 = $140
Lost revenue: $200 - $140 = $60

73. True

According to PGA Professional Craig Shankland, the maximum number of lessons an instructor should teach per day should not exceed 10 half-hour lessons, or 6 one-hour lessons.

74. B
The three elements used to evaluate whether a golf club will improve a player's performance are quality, design, and fit.

75. False
The flex characteristics of steel shafts are controlled primarily by wall thickness.

76. B
Graphite shafts transmit fewer vibrations up the shaft to a golfer's hands than steel shafts.

77. A
The thinner the shaft, the more torque it will have.

78. B
The thicker the shaft, the stiffer and heavier it will be.

79. B
The stiffness, flex points, and torque of graphite shafts are controlled by the fiber's tensile strength, the amount of fiber, and the pattern in which the fibers are applied.

80. True
To be legal for events played under USGA and R&A rules, all golf balls must pass a test on initial velocity, weight, size, symmetry of design pattern, and overall distance.

81. False
The distance a golf ball travels is affected by its size, weight, dimple design, and the material of its cover and core.

82. False
Golf ball performance is distinguished by compression, durability, material, and aerodynamics.

83. B
For iron shots, the clubhead should strike the ball with a descending arc.

84. B
For iron shots, the clubhead's center of gravity at impact should be equal to, or lower than, that of the center of gravity of the ball.

85. True
The golf course Superintendent is entrusted with the maintenance, operation, and management of a golf course.

86. B
The golf course Superintendent must achieve and document compliance with the EPA (Environmental Protection Agency) and OSHA (Occupational Safety and Health Administration).

87. False
The basic zones of turfgrass adaptation in the United States are cool season grass, warm season grass, and a transition zone.

88. B
There are 3 basic zones of turfgrass adaptation in the United States.

89. A
Northern climate grasses include bentgrass, bluegrass, ryegrass, and fescues.

90. C
Southern climate grasses include zoysiagrass, buffalograss, and bermudagrass.

91. C
Cool season grasses thrive in temperatures ranging from 60 to 75 degrees.

92. B
In areas that receive snow, cool season grasses become dormant and turn brown.

93. C
Warm season grasses thrive in temperatures ranging from 80 to 95 degrees.

94. C
There are 15 essential nutrients for turfgrass that occur naturally in sufficient quantities in the air. 3 essential nutrients (nitrogen, phosphorus, and potassium) may be supplemented through fertilizers.

95. C
In plants, the growing point is at the tip of the shoot. In grass, the growing point is at the base of the shoot.

96. D
Shoots need sunlight in order to produce food for the plant. Roots absorb water and nutrients.

97. False
Sandy soil allows water to pass through quickly, while clay soil tends to retain water.

98. B
Soil can be classified by the size of its particles.

99. B
Loam soil creates a stable growing environment for a plant by providing a balance between drainage and retention.

100. C
Sandy soil is composed of large particles that allow water and nutrients to pass through so quickly that they are not readily available for the plant.

101. True
Soil pH measures soil acidity and alkalinity.

102. C
On the soil pH scale, a measure of 0 is highly acidic, and a measure of 14 is highly alkaline.

103. A
Turfgrass grows best in soils that are slightly acidic.

104. True
Clay soil tends to be acidic.

105. False
Sandy soil tends to be alkaline.

106. A
Lime may be added to soil to raise its pH level.

107. B
Sulfur may be added to soil to lower its pH level.

108. C
A technique called syringing may be used to cool off turfgrass through a light application of water to the grass surface.

109. B
Syringing should be applied at the first sign of wilt.

110. A
During excessive heat, syringing may be applied up to 3 times daily.

111. False

Grasses that best tolerate shorter mowing heights are bermudagrass and bentgrass.

112. False

Longer grass tends to be healthier than shorter grass. Short heights are stressful for all types of grasses.

113. True

Ryegrass is commonly used as rough on a golf course because of its low maintenance requirements.

114. True

Removing the shoot reduces a plant's resistance to the invasion of disease.

115. False

Removing the shoot reduces a plant's ability to absorb water and nutrients.

116. False

Removing the shoot reduces a plant's ability to make its own food.

117. True

Grasses are able to regenerate their shoots if they are not cut too closely to their growing points.

118. C

The suggested mowing height for greens is 1/8" to 1/4".

119. B

The suggested mowing height for tees is 3/8" to 1".

120. B

The suggested mowing height for fairways is 1/2" to 1¼".

121. B

The suggested mowing height for rough is 2" or higher.

122. False

Shorter mowing heights create a turfgrass environment that requires more active maintenance.

123. True

Tees and fairways should be mowed 2 to 4 times per week depending on golf course conditions.

124. False
Greens can be mowed once or even twice per day, depending on golf course conditions.

125. D
A bag of fertilizer that reads 10-6-4 will contain 10% nitrogen, 6% phosphorus, and 4% potassium.

126. A
Soils are approximately 25% air, 25% water, and 50% solid.

127. True
Aeration involves removing 3 to 4 inches of soil from the ground.

128. False
Aeration stimulates the growth of new roots by increasing the air supply to the roots and allowing water and nutrients to penetrate into the root zone.

129. False
Aeration restores the passageways in soil that facilitate the flow of water, nutrients, and air to the plant.

130. True
Excess thatch prevents water, nutrients, fertilizers, and pesticides from penetrating into the soil and plant roots.

131. B
Topdressing is the practice of placing a layer of soil over the putting surface to smooth and decrease surface irregularity.

132. False
Topdressing is often performed immediately after aerating in order to fill holes created by aeration.

133. B
Overseeding is primarily used in southern areas of the country.

134. A
Overseeding involves planting cool season grasses over warm season grasses.

135. True
For insect prevention on turfgrass, thatch should be kept at a minimum.

136. False

The three broad categories of pests found on golf courses are insects, weeds, and diseases.

137. True

A weed is simply defined as a plant in an undesired location.

138. B

A herbicide should be used to kill unwanted plants on a golf course.

139. False

Integrated Pest Management (IPM) places an emphasis on prevention, rather than eradication. According to IPM, the Superintendent should take appropriate, but minimum action at first, and only take additional action if necessary.

140. False

Thick thatch prevents essential nutrients and insecticides from reaching the turfgrass, reducing its overall health.

141. C

Soil compaction occurs when the weight of heavy machinery compresses soil and causes a loss of pore space. Soil compaction may also occur due to lack of water in the soil.

142. True

Plants are classified by their lifecycle and plant structure.

143. D

Armyworms, sod webworms, and vegetable weevils are common surface insects found on a golf course. White grubs are subsurface insects.

144. B

Bermudagrass mites, centipedes, and nematodes are common subsurface insects found on a golf course. Chinch bugs are surface insects.

145. True

Overall thinning of turf is a warning sign that subsurface insects may be present.

146. A

Turf that is beginning to die along curbs or sidewalks, even with adequate watering, is an indication that surface insects may be present.

147. B
Turfgrass disease is primarily a result of fungi.

148. D
Thatch is a layer of organic matter that accumulates just below the grass blades and above the soil surface. Thatch may be harmful and should be removed.

149. B
Brown patch and dollar spot are common turfgrass diseases found on a golf course.

150. D
Fairy ring, grease spot (Pythium blight), and dollar spot are common turfgrass diseases found on a golf course.

151. False
The Superintendent is responsible for overseeing a turfgrass management program that provides a playing surface that meets the golf club's aesthetic and playing standards, while at the same time preserving the natural environment.

152. True
The Superintendent's responsibilities include managing the golf course, grounds surrounding the golf course, practice putting greens, golf range, parking lot, and entrance road.

153. C
The Superintendent is responsible for hiring, training, evaluating, and managing the year-round and seasonal maintenance staff.

154. D
The five phases of golf course design are:
Phase I: Site analysis
Phase II: Design
Phase III: Development
Phase IV: Grow-in
Phase V: Maintenance

155. A
The five phases of golf course design are:
Phase I: Site analysis
Phase II: Design
Phase III: Development
Phase IV: Grow-in
Phase V: Maintenance

156. B

The site analysis phase (Phase I) of the golf course design process takes approximately 4 to 6 months to complete.

157. C

The design phase (Phase II) of the golf course design process takes approximately 6 to 18 months to complete.

158. D

The development phase (Phase III) of the golf course design process takes approximately 12 to 18 months to complete.

159. A

The grow-in phase (Phase IV) of the golf course design process takes approximately 3 to 10 months to complete.

160. C

In Phase II of the golf course design process, the proper steps placed in the correct order are: base map, routing plan, concept plan, and construction plan.

161. A

The base map, as part of the golf course design process, should include underground utilities, right-of-ways, structures, historical sites, and environmental resources such as wetlands.

162. True

The routing plan, as part of the golf course design process, may also be referred to as a schematic.

163. C

The first step to developing a routing plan is to identify possible locations for the clubhouse. Then, at each potential clubhouse location, a practice facility site should be identified.

164. D

The concept plan provides a visual image of how a golf course will look once it is complete.

165. D

The concept plan displays the shape, size, and form of each golf course feature, including tees, greens, bunkers, and hazards.

166. A

A construction plan guides the building of a golf course. It includes specific plans for irrigation, landscaping, grading, and other course features.

167. C
Finalizing the construction plan marks the end of the golf course design phase (Phase II), and provides the basis for the development phase (Phase III).

168. True
The development phase (Phase III) of the golf course design process includes seven steps in the following order: staking, clearing, rough grading and major drainage, feature construction and minor drainage, irrigation, finished grading and planting preparation, and planting.

169. B
Major earth moving occurs during the "rough grading and major drainage" step of the golf course development phase (Phase III).

170. C
Small bulldozers shape the final form of the golf course as part of the "feature construction and minor drainage" step of the golf course development phase (Phase III).

171. True
Golf course irrigation systems may be automatic or manual, single line or double line, electrical or hydraulic.

172. False
When planting a newly developed golf course, the tees and greens should be planted first, then fairways, and finally the rough.

173. False
The grow-in period of golf course design can take 3 to 10 months to complete, depending on the climate and weather.

174. B
The members of the core team responsible for designing and developing a golf course are the architect, Superintendent, and contractor.

175. D
The contractor is typically hired at the end of the golf course design phase (Phase II) through a bidding process.

176. B
The Superintendent assumes the lead at the end of the development phase (Phase III), and consults with the architect as needed.

177. B

The Head Professional works most closely with the Superintendent during the golf course design process.

178. C

Land planners, environmentalists, hydrologists, archaeologists, legal counsel, and financial advisors are employed during the site analysis phase (Phase I) of the golf course design process.

179. A

Interior designers, publicists, landscape architects, and building architects are employed during the design phase (Phase II) of the golf course design process.

180. D

Bricklayers, concrete pourers, irrigation specialists, and heavy equipment operators are employed during the development phase (Phase III) of the golf course design process.

181. True

Surface drainage is the slope and shape of the land.

182. True

Subsurface drainage is the internal drainage of the soil.

183. False

Subsurface drainage is primarily a function of soil content.

184. False

Surface drainage is primarily a function of the land's topography.

185. False

Subsurface drainage systems are typically used in areas of a golf course that require the highest level of maintenance, such as tees and greens.

186. C

Soil amendments and construction of drainage systems are methods used to create adequate subsurface drainage.

187. True

When constructing greens, use layered soils with a combination of coarse and fine textures to produce a balance between retention and drainage.

188. B
The modern methods of constructing greens are the California Greens Construction Method, Topsoil Greens Construction Method, and the USGA Greens Construction Method.

189. C
The tee area for each hole should be at least 6,000 square feet, which is large enough to allow for frequent movement of tee markers.

190. A
Because they receive more wear, the first, tenth, and par-3 tees usually average 8,000 square feet or more.

191. B
Greens sizes typically range from 5,000 to 8,000 square feet at a PGA recognized golf course.

192. C
There should be a 12 to 15 foot collar around the perimeter of each green where no cups should be placed.

193. B
A green should have 12 to 20 areas for possible cup placement, with a 3 foot radius around the cup with no slope.

194. True
The landing area following a tee shot should be at least 200 to 250 square feet at a minimum.

195. False
Adjacent tees and greens should be 100 feet apart at their borders, and 200 feet apart from their center points.

196. A
Golf holes should be routed clockwise to allow right-handed golfers to slice into the course, not out of bounds.

197. True
The recreational golf experience is divided into five phases: anticipation, arrival, participation, cool down, and memory.

198. A
A penal golf hole design is not forgiving because it leaves little room for error. A heroic golf hole requires extraordinary maneuvers.

199. A
The golfer should be able to view the entire hole from the tee-off position. The contour of the tee area should direct the golfer towards the intended line of play.

200. False
Hazards should be used to direct play, and provide depth perception, variety, and challenge.

LEVEL 3

QUESTIONS

1. Which of the following is a type of budget plan that helps a golf professional determine how much money should be spent on merchandise classifications, and also tracks how much money will remain each month to buy or restock inventory?

   A. COGS plan
   B. OTB plan
   C. POS plan
   D. MAP plan

2. Small golf shops typically have at least _____ merchandise classifications. Large golf shops have _____ or more merchandise classifications.

   A. 5, 40
   B. 10, 40
   C. 10, 20
   D. 20, 40

3. In an OTB plan, all dollars should be committed to use at all times in order to maximize returns.

   True
   False

4. Cost of goods sold is the wholesale price vendors charge for merchandise. It excludes merchandise that is lost or stolen.

   True
   False

5. Cost of goods sold may include additional costs such as shipping, ticketing, and handling.

True
False

6. Which of the following formulas is used to calculate cost of goods sold (COGS)?

   A. COGS = beginning of month inventory + purchases − end of month inventory
   B. COGS = beginning of month inventory − purchases − end of month inventory
   C. COGS = beginning of month inventory + purchases + end of month inventory
   D. COGS = beginning of month inventory − purchases + end of month inventory

7. Calculate the cost of goods sold if the beginning of month inventory was $40,000, the end of month inventory was $70,000, and there were $50,000 of purchases made during the month.

   A. $10,000
   B. $20,000
   C. $30,000
   D. $40,000

8. Cost of goods sold as a percentage of sales should be between 50% and 60% for hard goods, and between 65% and 75% for soft goods.

True
False

9. Goods that are immediately consumed in one use are considered which of the following?

   A. Soft goods
   B. Hard goods
   C. Durable goods
   D. None of the above

10. The higher a golf shop's inventory turnover rate, the _____ inventory is needed on hand to reach the same sales goals.

    A. More
    B. Less

11. Which of the following formulas is used to calculate the average monthly inventory level?

    A. Average monthly inventory level = turnover rate / annual COGS
    B. Average monthly inventory level = annual COGS x turnover rate
    C. Average monthly inventory level = annual COGS / turnover rate
    D. Average monthly inventory level = (annual COGS − turnover rate) / annual COGS

12. Determine the average monthly inventory level for The Golf Shop, if the monthly cost of goods sold is $20,000, and the turnover rate is 2.5.

    A. $8,000
    B. $16,000
    C. $48,000
    D. $96,000

13. The average turnover rate for all golf shops is _____. The average turnover rate for private equity PGA facilities is _____.

    A. 2.5, 1.5
    B. 1.5, 2.5
    C. 3.6, 4.0
    D. 4.0, 3.6

14. The average turnover rate for all sporting retailers is _____. The average turnover rate for top golf merchandisers is _____.

    A. 2.5, 1.5
    B. 1.5, 2.5
    C. 3.6, 4.0
    D. 4.0, 3.6

15. The highest turnover items at both private and municipal golf facilities are shoes and outerwear.

    True
    False

16. An excessively high turnover rate can lead to a higher cost of goods sold percentage.

    True
    False

17. Which of the following is/are correct regarding seasonal and monthly sales fluctuations?

    (1) Inventory levels should increase one month before the peak season begins.
    (2) Enough inventory should be on hand at the beginning of the season to cover sales for approximately 90 days.

    A. (1) only
    B. (2) only
    C. All of the above
    D. None of the above

18. Which of the following plans establishes the quantity, sizes, colors, materials, models, styles, types of brands, and planned price points for each product line?

    A. Cost of goods sold plan
    B. Open-to-buy plan
    C. Gross profit margin plan
    D. Merchandise assortment plan

19. The MAP process includes reviewing the needs of customers, evaluating previous year performance by merchandise classification, researching market trends, and selecting the merchandise mix to purchase.

    True
    False

20. Which of the following billing strategies involves setting a future date when payment is due, and offering a discount for early payment?

A. Spring dating
B. Collaborative dating
C. Anticipation dating
D. None of the above

21. If a golf shop receives merchandise in the fall of the current year, with payment due in April or May of the following year, which type of billing strategy is being used?

A. Spring dating
B. Collaborative dating
C. Anticipation dating
D. None of the above

22. All but which of the following are advantages to using extended billing strategies?

A. Higher inventory levels
B. Opportunity to sell item's at no immediate cost
C. Reduced number of back orders
D. All of the above are advantages to using extended billing.

23. Successful golf shops use multiple vendors to increase diversification and product selection. It's common for a golf shop to work with hundreds of different vendors at any given time.

True
False

24. Which of the following markup approaches is often used at private facilities, and involves members paying an initial fee at the beginning of the season which allows them to purchase merchandise at a small percentage above cost?

A. Keystoning
B. MSRP
C. Cost plus markup
D. Mill River Plan

25. **Which of the following markup approaches doubles an item's cost to arrive at the final retail price?**

   A. Keystoning
   B. MSRP
   C. Cost plus markup
   D. Mill River Plan

26. **Which of the following markup approaches uses a target markup percentage as the basis for pricing merchandise?**

   A. Keystoning
   B. MSRP
   C. Cost plus markup
   D. Mill River Plan

27. **According to the keystoning approach to product markups, if a pair of golf shoes was purchased from a vendor for $85, what will be the final retail price? Assume the MSRP is $190.**

   A. $95
   B. $170
   C. $190
   D. Cannot be determined from the information provided

28. **If a golf shop sets merchandise prices according to the manufacturer's suggested retail price, the golf shop will usually lower the price of _____ before lowering the price of _____.**

   A. Soft goods, Hard goods
   B. Hard goods, Soft goods

29. **All but which of the following are competitive factors that influence price markup?**

   A. Exclusivity
   B. Follow the leader
   C. Opportunistic pricing
   D. Convenience

30. All but which of the following are value added factors that influence price markup?

A. Product availability
B. Facility image
C. Supply and demand
D. Services

31. All but which of the following are consequences of poor pricing?

A. Lost sales
B. Failure to reach financial goals
C. Excess inventory
D. Excessive turnover

32. Which of the following is an inventory control tool used to identify what merchandise is on order, when it was ordered, who ordered it, and when it will be delivered?

A. OTB
B. MAP
C. PO
D. POS

33. Which of the following formulas is used to calculate a product's markup percentage?

A. Markup % = markup x cost
B. Markup % = markup / cost
C. Markup % = cost / markup
D. Markup % = (markup − cost) / cost

34. If a product's markup is $18, and the original cost of the product was $26, what is the markup percentage?

A. 53%
B. 58%
C. 65%
D. 69%

35. If a product's markup is $12, and the final retail price of the product is $44, what is the gross margin %?

A. 9%
B. 18%
C. 27%
D. 36%

36. When pricing merchandise, a golf professional should establish gross margin goals first, and then determine what the product markup should be in order to achieve it.

True
False

37. A golf facility's actual gross margin will be _____ markup because some items will be marked down, lost, stolen, or damaged.

A. Less than
B. Greater than
C. Equal to
D. Greater than or equal to

38. Calculate total revenue per round for The Golf Club, which had total monthly revenue of $80,000, and of that amount 60% was attributed to greens fees. There were 1,300 rounds of golf played during the month.

A. $24.62
B. $36.92
C. $61.54
D. $68.10

39. Calculate merchandise revenue per round for The Golf Club, which had total monthly revenue of $80,000, and of that amount 20% was attributed to merchandise sales. There were 1,300 rounds of golf played during the month.

   A. $12.31
   B. $22.12
   C. $49.23
   D. $61.54

40. Supply and demand are competitive factors that affect a golf shop's pricing strategy.

   True
   False

41. Which of the following is a golf shop floor plan that illustrates where different types of merchandise should be placed?

   A. Mapogram
   B. Destination map
   C. Planogram
   D. Merchandise map

42. There are only four key elements involved in creating an attractive buying environment for customers. They are signage, lighting, staff selling skills, and fixtures.

   True
   False

43. In general, a golf shop should not be departmentalized. Instead the floor layout should be open with a mixture of merchandise throughout the golf shop.

   True
   False

44. Attention-getting displays in a golf shop create changing elevations, highlight a coordinated look, and make merchandise easily accessible.

   True
   False

45. When hanging merchandise in a golf shop, size items from _____, beginning with the smallest size and increasing size as you move to the _____.

   A. Right to left, Left
   B. Left to right, Right

46. When displaying folded merchandise, size items from _____, beginning with the smallest size and increasing size as you move to the _____.

   A. Top to bottom, Bottom
   B. Bottom to top, Top

47. Flexible fixtures in a golf shop should present older merchandise in a new light, keep the golf shop looking full when inventory is low, and enhance the golf shop's image.

   True
   False

48. Which of the following systems automatically updates a golf shop's open-to-buy plan, allows for timely reporting of sales information, helps with price control, and maintains an accurate inventory?

   A. OTB system
   B. MAP system
   C. PO system
   D. POS system

49. **"Destination items" are products that customers intend to purchase before entering the golf shop.**

   True
   False

50. **A golf professional should clean displays and mirrors, vacuum the floor, and organize the counter area _____. He or she should organize the back room, wipe down shelves, and clean air vents _____.**

   A. Hourly, Weekly
   B. Daily, Monthly
   C. Weekly, Monthly
   D. Daily, Weekly

51. **Which of the following lists the six steps of event preparation in the correct order?**

   A. Set objectives, decide requirements, identify tasks, establish budget, communicate plan, schedule activities
   B. Establish budget, set objectives, identify tasks, decide requirements, schedule activities, communicate plan
   C. Set objectives, establish budget, decide requirements, identify tasks, schedule activities, communicate plan
   D. Establish budget, decide requirements, set objectives, identify tasks, communicate plan, schedule activities

52. **The five steps of the selling process in the correct order are: collect key information, approach the customer, present merchandise, close the sale, and build future sales.**

   True
   False

53. A physical inventory count should be performed at least _____ per year.

A. Once
B. Twice
C. Three times
D. Four times

54. A perpetual book inventory system tracks changes to merchandise levels, both in terms of dollar value and number of units, on a daily basis or as they occur.

True
False

55. Physical unit inventory tracking indicates the dollar value of inventory on hand and sold, and the history of price changes and markdowns.

True
False

56. Which inventory tracking method indicates the quantity of merchandise on hand, sold, and on order, and the age of the merchandise?

A. FIFO inventory tracking
B. Financial value inventory tracking
C. Perpetual book inventory tracking
D. Physical unit inventory tracking

57. All but which of the following are advantages of high merchandise turnover?

A. Higher cost of goods sold percentage
B. Fewer markdowns
C. Better ROI
D. Increased ability to capitalize on new trends

58. The gross profit margin for a public golf facility should be at least _____. The gross profit margin for a private golf facility should be at least _____.

A. 10%, 40%
B. 30%, 50%
C. 40%, 10%
D. 50%, 30%

59. The Golf Shop had $83,250 total cost of goods sold for the year. The average inventory at cost was $51,400. What was the inventory turnover rate?

A. 1.49
B. 1.55
C. 1.62
D. 1.68

60. Which of the following formulas is used to calculate average inventory at cost?

A. Average inventory at cost = total end of month inventory on hand / length of season
B. Average inventory at cost = length of season / total end of month inventory on hand
C. Average inventory at cost = total end of month inventory on hand x length of season
D. Average inventory at cost = total end of month inventory on hand − length of season

61. Gross margin return on investment (GMROI) calculates the profit made for each dollar spent on inventory.

True
False

62. Golf shops that achieve a GMROI of 40% to 60% are considered to be performing very well.

True
False

63. Gross margin is defined as the difference between total merchandise sales and the cost of goods sold.

True
False

64. Which of the following allows a golf professional to measure the true profitability of different products, such as those that have high margins (golf shoes) and those that have high turnover (golf tees)?

A. COGS
B. ROI
C. GMROI
D. OTB

65. To successfully manage a golf shop, a golf professional should do which of the following?

A. Track sales performance
B. Analyze variances in sales
C. Adjust factors as needed
D. All of the above

66. Point-of-sale markdowns are permanent reductions in list price and should be indicated on merchandise tags.

True
False

67. Which of the following is a partnership building process that empowers employees?

A. Supervising
B. Directing
C. Delegating
D. Supporting

68. **Delegating is, by its nature, a technique used by managers to control employees.**

True
False

69. **Two key factors a manager should consider before delegating an assignment to an employee are _____ and _____.**

A. Time, Willingness
B. Time, Capabilities
C. Capabilities, Results
D. Capabilities, Willingness

70. **Which interaction strategy should be used by a manager if an employee is resistant and experienced?**

A. Directing
B. Involving
C. Convincing
D. Supporting

71. **Which interaction strategy should be used by a manager if an employee is enthusiastic and inexperienced?**

A. Directing
B. Involving
C. Convincing
D. Supporting

72. **Which interaction strategy should be used by a manager if an employee is enthusiastic and experienced?**

A. Directing
B. Involving
C. Convincing
D. Supporting

73. **Which interaction strategy should be used by a manager if an employee is resistant and inexperienced?**

A. Directing
B. Involving
C. Convincing
D. Supporting

74. **Which of the following is/are the basic means available to support an employee in completing a task?**

A. Feedback
B. Inventory
C. Resources
D. Input

75. **Which of the following is/are the information, circumstances, or events that prompt an employee to take action to complete a task?**

A. Input
B. Resources
C. Feedback
D. Consequences

76. **Which of the following is/are the specific information an employee receives about the results of his or her actions?**

A. Consequences
B. Resources
C. Feedback
D. Input

77. All but which of the following are among the building blocks to creating motivating work?

   A. The work assignment
   B. The performer
   C. The work environment
   D. The reward for completion

78. All but which of the following are among the five principles of motivating work?

   A. Significant work
   B. Autonomy
   C. Compensation
   D. Feedback

79. All but which of the following are among the five principles of motivating work?

   A. Skill variety
   B. Accommodations
   C. Whole task
   D. Autonomy

80. Autonomy is allowing staff members to decide how best to complete a task.

   True
   False

81. If a staff member has autonomy, he or she is responsible for completing the entire task from beginning to end.

   True
   False

82. A/An _____ makes a manager's input even more obvious and understandable to an employee.

A. Task amplifier
B. Input modifier
C. Task modifier
D. Input amplifier

83. Which principle of motivating work is being used when a manager reorganizes tasks around natural and complete units of work?

A. Skill variety
B. Significant work
C. Whole task
D. Autonomy

84. Which principle of motivating work is being used when a manager looks for opportunities to build into a job the type of work an employee wants to do?

A. Skill variety
B. Autonomy
C. Feedback
D. Significant work

85. Four ways a manager can make performance problems worse are inaction, wrong assumptions, confrontation, and failure to involve the employee.

True
False

86. Which of the following is the first stage of the four-stage sequence for correcting performance problems?

A. Reinforced problem solving with the performer
B. Joint problem solving with the performer
C. Termination of the employment relationship
D. Final decision making with the performer

87. Which of the following is the second stage of the four-stage sequence for correcting performance problems?

A. Reinforced problem solving with the performer
B. Joint problem solving with the performer
C. Termination of the employment relationship
D. Final decision making with the performer

88. Which of the following is the third stage of the four-stage sequence for correcting performance problems?

A. Reinforced problem solving with the performer
B. Joint problem solving with the performer
C. Termination of the employment relationship
D. Final decision making with the performer

89. Which of the following is the fourth stage of the four-stage sequence for correcting performance problems?

A. Reinforced problem solving with the performer
B. Joint problem solving with the performer
C. Termination of the employment relationship
D. Final decision making with the performer

90. In which stage of the four-stage sequence for correcting performance problems will the manager insist on the need to resolve the performance problem, and re-emphasize the importance of the performer's role in the resolution process?

A. Stage 1
B. Stage 2
C. Stage 3
D. Stage 4

91. Which interaction strategy is most likely to be used in the third stage of the four-stage sequence for correcting performance problems?

    A. Directing
    B. Convincing
    C. Involving
    D. Supporting

92. In which stage of the four-stage sequence for correcting performance problems will the manager ask the employee for ideas on how to solve the problem?

    A. Stage 1
    B. Stage 2
    C. Stage 3
    D. Stage 4

93. Which of the following is/are correct regarding a golf instructor's teaching philosophy?

    (1) A teaching philosophy summarizes an instructor's views, beliefs, concepts, and attitudes towards the game of golf and how it should be taught.
    (2) A teaching philosophy is essentially an instructor's mission statement.

    A. (1) only
    B. (2) only
    C. All of the above
    D. None of the above

94. Which of the following individuals is famously quoted as saying that putting is the "game within a game"?

    A. Walter Travis
    B. Percy Boomer
    C. Jerry Travers
    D. Harry Vardon

95. Putting strokes account for approximately 20% of all strokes taken during a round of golf for a low handicap player.

True
False

96. Proper putting technique suggests a golfer's eye line should be directly over, or slightly inside, the ball.

True
False

97. Which of the following is the most common putting grip?

A. Overlap
B. Reverse overlap
C. Interlock
D. Cross-handed

98. All but which of the following are among the goals of selecting the proper putting grip?

A. Resist wristiness
B. Resist clubface rotation
C. Promote clubface rotation
D. None of the above

99. For the proper putting setup, the ball should be forward of center and the eye line should be directly behind the ball.

True
False

100. The average loft of a putter is 4.0 degrees, and the average lie is 73.5 degrees. The average putter length is 35.5 inches, and the average weight is 11.5 ounces.

True
False

101. For long distance putts, the goal is to have the next putt be _____ or less.

A. 6 inches
B. 1 foot
C. 3 feet
D. 6 feet

102. Which of the following types of grass has the most grain?

A. Bermudagrass
B. Ryegrass
C. Bentgrass
D. Buffalograss

103. A shiny putting surface means the grain is going _____ the golfer. A dull surface means the grain is going _____ the golfer.

A. Towards, Away from
B. Away from, Towards

104. Which of the following rules of thumb for putting is/are correct?

(1) 60% of a putt's break will occur within three feet of the hole.
(2) Grain usually affects only the last foot of role.

A. (1) only
B. (2) only
C. All of the above
D. None of the above

105. Which of the following rules of thumb for putting is/are correct?

(1) **X-out golf balls are poorly balanced for putting, and can affect a 6-foot putt by as many as 3 or 4 inches.**
(2) **A 2.5 foot putt has an alignment error of +/- 10 degrees.**

A. (1) only
B. (2) only
C. All of the above
D. None of the above

106. **The distinguishing factor between a chip and a pitch is that a chip is a two-lever stroke (cocked wrists), and a pitch is a one-lever stroke (firm wrists).**

True
False

107. **The preferred method of transitioning from chipping to pitching is moving the ball to the centerline of the body using a wedge.**

True
False

108. **Which of the following is/are correct regarding proper grip pressure when chipping and pitching?**

(1) **Grip pressure may be firm or light, but should never be tight.**
(2) **Lighter grip pressure slows clubhead speed, and firmer grip pressure increases it.**

A. (1) only
B. (2) only
C. All of the above
D. None of the above

109. All but which of the following are reasons why a golfer's feet and hips should be open when chipping and pitching?

   A. Easier to see the target
   B. Causes the backswing to be more on target
   C. Easier to swing to the target
   D. Causes less restriction on the backswing

110. When chipping and pitching from a bare lie, move the ball _____ in stance. For a fluffy lie move the ball _____ in stance.

   A. Forward, Back
   B. Back, Forward

111. When chipping and pitching, move the ball _____ in stance to produce a higher trajectory. Move the ball _____ in stance to produce a lower trajectory.

   A. Forward, Back
   B. Back, Forward

112. The vertical centerline of a golfer's body should be 2 inches in front of the ball for a pitch, and even for a chip.

   True
   False

113. A useful phrase to recite when teaching the principles of chipping and pitching is, "The left hand should never stop moving towards the target."

   True
   False

114. All but which of the following are proper techniques for hitting a cut shot?

   A. Open the clubface
   B. Aim left
   C. Keep the hands and arms back
   D. Keep the body back

115. To hit a cut-lob shot, move the ball forward in stance, open the clubface, and swing with the arms.

   True
   False

116. All but which of the following are proper techniques for hitting a flop shot?

   A. Allow the left wrist to break downward.
   B. Strike the ball with a steep descent..
   C. Maintain wristy action through the golf ball.
   D. All of the above are proper techniques for hitting a flop shot.

117. A sand wedge has all but which of the following features intended to help easily remove the ball from a greenside bunker?

   A. Reduced swing weight
   B. Camber
   C. Sole inversion
   D. Breadth

118. Which of the following terms describes the curvature of a golf club's sole?

   A. Depth
   B. Breadth
   C. Camber
   D. Sole inversion

119. **Which of the following terms describes the width of a golf club's sole?**

    A. Depth
    B. Breadth
    C. Camber
    D. Sole inversion

120. **Which of the following individuals is credited with inventing the modern sand wedge?**

    A. Harvey Penick
    B. Gene Sarazan
    C. Ben Hogan
    D. Sam Snead

121. **For greenside bunker shots, _____ is promoted if the heel of the golf club leads. _____ is promoted if the toe of the golf club leads.**

    A. Dig, Camber
    B. Bounce, Dig
    C. Camber, Bounce
    D. Dig, Bounce

122. **Camber helps irons dig _____ into the ground when taking divots.**

    A. More
    B. Less

123. **Sole inversion is caused by the bottom of a golf club's sole being lower than the leading edge.**

    True
    False

124. **Which of the following is/are correct regarding the proper method of playing a buried greenside bunker shot?**

(1) Move the ball forward in stance to increase penetration with the clubface.
(2) Turn the toe of the clubhead in for a knife-like leading edge to penetrate through the sand more easily.

A. (1) only
B. (2) only
C. All of the above
D. None of the above

125. **For bunker shots, a _____ angle of approach will make the ball travel a shorter a distance than a _____ angle of approach with the same effort.**

A. Steep, Shallow
B. Shallow, Steep

126. **For a greenside bunker shot, the ball should be played 4 to 6 inches _____ of the golfer's vertical centerline.**

A. Left
B. Right

127. **For a greenside bunker shot, a "U" shaped swing will produce a higher and softer shot. A "V" shaped swing will hit the ball lower and further with the same effort.**

True
False

128. **Always contact the sand first when hitting from a fairway bunker.**

True
False

129. As a rule of thumb, a golfer should choke down on the club as far down as his feet are buried into the sand for a fairway bunker shot.

True
False

130. For fairway bunker shots, firm sand requires _____ bounce. Soft sand requires _____ bounce.

A. More, Less
B. Less, More

131. "Balancing a glass of water on the clubface" is a useful visual image to teach students in order to keep them from closing the clubface during greenside bunker shots.

True
False

132. For a sidehill lie with the ball above the feet, a golfer's tendency will be all but which of the following?

A. Chunking
B. Pulling
C. Topping
D. Hooking

133. For a sidehill lie with the ball above the feet, the golfer should stand as _____ to the lie as possible.

A. Perpendicular
B. Parallel

134. For a sidehill lie with the ball below the feet, a golfer's tendency will be all but which of the following?

A. Chunking
B. Pushing
C. Topping
D. Slicing

135. For an uphill lie, a golfer's tendency will be all but which of the following?

A. Chunking
B. Pulling
C. Hitting behind the ball
D. Pushing

136. For an uphill lie, the golfer should lean away from the hill in order to resist gravity's pull.

True
False

137. A punch shot is effective into the wind because it produces increased backspin and causes the ball to upshoot.

True
False

138. For a downhill lie, a golfer's tendency will be all but which of the following?

A. Topping
B. Chunking
C. Pushing
D. Hitting behind the ball

139. To hook the golf ball, sole the clubface square and use a closed face grip. Aim the feet and shoulders to the left of the target.

   True
   False

140. A semi-private teaching lesson includes how many students?

   A. 2 to 4
   B. 5 more
   C. 8 to 12
   D. 10 or more

141. A group lesson should be limited to 5 to 12 students in total. This allows 3 to 5 minutes each for individual instruction.

   True
   False

142. Which of the following includes a blend of demonstration, observation, and coaching students while they hit golf balls?

   A. Demonstration clinic
   B. Participation clinic
   C. Group lesson
   D. Golf school

143. The purpose of a _____ is to educate and entertain students by blending fun with fundamentals.

   A. Demonstration clinic
   B. Participation clinic
   C. Group lesson
   D. Golf school

144. A demonstration clinic should be limited to 90 minutes if the audience is seated.

   True
   False

145. When hosting a golf school, the maximum student-teacher ratio should not exceed which of the following?

   A. 4 to 1
   B. 8 to 1
   C. 12 to 1
   D. 20 to 1

146. All but which of the following are basic body types?

   A. Ectomorph
   B. Peramorph
   C. Mesomorph
   D. Endomorph

147. Which of the following body types is characterized by small bones, low muscle tone, and a frame that is soft and round? Individuals with this body type are generally poor athletes.

   A. Ectomorph
   B. Peramorph
   C. Mesomorph
   D. Endomorph

148. Which of the following body types is characterized by thin muscles, thin bones, a short trunk, and long arms and legs? Individuals with this body type generally have high endurance levels.

   A. Ectomorph
   B. Peramorph
   C. Mesomorph
   D. Endomorph

149. Which of the following body types is characterized by large muscles, big bones, broad shoulders, and a slender waist? Individuals with this body type generally have increased strength.

A. Ectomorph
B. Peramorph
C. Mesomorph
D. Endomorph

150. Golfers who are tall in stature generally have good balance, a flat swing, a shallow angle of approach, and tend to draw the ball.

True
False

151. Senior golfers who are losing strength and range of motion should adopt a more clockwise-positioned grip to reduce forearm and hand rotation.

True
False

152. Learning golf's history, traditions, rules, and etiquette should not be the primary focus of a group lesson for junior golfers. Instead an emphasis should be placed on having fun in order to make the junior golfers lifelong participants in the sport.

True
False

153. The ideal ages to learn the golf swing are between _____ years old.

A. 8 and 12
B. 13 and 20
C. 21 and 30
D. 31 and 40

154. While 10% to 15% of Americans are left-handed, only 3% to 6% play golf left-handed.

    True
    False

155. A right-handed golf instructor should use himself as a mirror image when teaching swing fundamentals to a left-handed student.

    True
    False

156. Which of the following are the four basic fitness components that affect a golfer's skill level?

    A. Bend, reach, torque, endurance
    B. Mind, body, spirit, coordination
    C. Strength, flexibility, muscular endurance, neuromuscular coordination
    D. Strength, flexibility, muscular endurance, cardiovascular endurance

157. A successful food and beverage operation should be flexible and follow the acronym PACE, which stands for primary plan, alternative plan, contingency plan, and emergency plan.

    True
    False

158. Which of the following is/are correct regarding the difference between strategies and objectives in the food and beverage industry?

    (1) An example of an objective in the food and beverage industry is to establish and grow profit for the long-term.
    (2) Objectives are the steps required to connect tangible actions with intangible strategies.

    A. (1) only
    B. (2) only
    C. All of the above
    D. None of the above

159. Which of the following terms means to follow the golf facility's predetermined standards, while exercising restraint over the price the facility pays to purchase, prepare, and sell food?

    A. Linear food cost analysis
    B. Food and beverage mission statement
    C. Food cost control
    D. None of the above

160. Food cost control can be applied to areas such as purchasing, receiving, and service, but not to areas such as the storeroom and menu.

    True
    False

161. What percentage of a golf facility's non-dues related income should come from food and beverage operations?

    A. At least 50%
    B. At least 30%
    C. At least 5%
    D. At least 75%

162. The primary goal of successful food and beverage operations is to achieve total customer satisfaction.

    True
    False

163. All but which of the following are among the three basic types of golf facilities?

    A. Public
    B. Private
    C. Semi-private
    D. Equity

164. **All but which of the following are among the three basic types of private golf facilities?**

    A. Developer-owned
    B. Equity
    C. Debt financed
    D. Privately managed

165. **Which type of private golf facility is owned by its members? Service, not profit, is the operational goal.**

    A. Developer-owned
    B. Equity
    C. Debt financed
    D. Privately managed

166. **Which type of private golf facility has high profit and full membership as its primary goals?**

    A. Developer-owned
    B. Equity
    C. Debt financed
    D. Privately managed

167. **There are only four levels of food and beverage service in the golf industry. They are on-course concessions, carryout, full service, and formal fine dining.**

    True
    False

168. **Which of the following is the easiest and least expensive level of food and beverage service because it requires minimal staff and equipment?**

    A. On-course concessions
    B. Carryout
    C. Full service
    D. Formal fine dining

169. **Which of the following is the most basic and important control tool used in a food and beverage operation?**

A. Price
B. Menu
C. Customer surveys
D. Competitors

170. **Which of the following lists the four steps of menu development in the correct order?**

A. Develop menu concept, determine menu costs, develop and test recipes, print menu and train staff
B. Develop menu concept, print menu and train staff, determine menu costs, develop and test recipes
C. Develop menu concept, develop and test recipes, determine menu costs, print menu and train staff
D. Determine menu costs, develop menu concept, develop and test recipes, print menu and train staff

171. **Which of the following is the blueprint used to develop a food and beverage item?**

A. Portion size
B. Standard recipe
C. Menu
D. Nutritional values

172. **A "picture board" should be maintained in the kitchen to demonstrate the standard plate presentation.**

True
False

173. The Food and Beverage Director should cost all menu items _____ to ensure they remain within budgeted goals.

   A. Weekly
   B. Monthly
   C. Quarterly
   D. Annually

174. Which of the following formulas is used to calculate the standard portion cost of a menu item?

   A. Standard portion cost = total cost of recipe / number of portions
   B. Standard portion cost = total cost of recipe x number of portions
   C. Standard portion cost = number of portions / total cost of recipe
   D. Standard portion cost = (number of portions − total cost of recipe) / number of portions

175. If the total cost of a lobster recipe is $440, and the recipe serves 40 customers, what is the standard portion cost?

   A. $8
   B. $11
   C. $16
   D. $20

176. To determine a menu item's base selling price, multiply the entrée cost by the price multiplier. The price multiplier is equal to 100% divided by the food cost goal.

   True
   False

177. If a restaurant's food cost goal is 28%, and a menu item costs $2.95, what is the item's base selling price?

   A. $9.44
   B. $9.72
   C. $9.99
   D. $10.53

178. Which of the following is the primary goal of identifying appropriate staffing levels for a food and beverage operation?

    A. Achieve total customer satisfaction
    B. Maximize profit
    C. Balance customer service with payroll efficiency
    D. Low employee turnover

179. Which of the following is/are correct regarding the appropriate staffing levels for a food and beverage operation?

    (1) For on-course concessions, there should be 1 attendant per 50 to 60 rounds of golf.
    (2) For carryout service, there should be 1 attendant per 20 to 30 rounds of golf per hour.

    A. (1) only
    B. (2) only
    C. All of the above
    D. None of the above

180. For a full service food and beverage operation, there should be 1 server and cook per 6 customers per hour. There should be 1 bartender/washer/host/busser per 2 to 3 servers.

    True
    False

181. For formal fine dining, there should be 1 cook per _____ customers.

    A. 6
    B. 8
    C. 10
    D. 12

182. **For formal fine dining, there should be 1 front server per _____ customers.**

    A. 6
    B. 8
    C. 10
    D. 12

183. **Which of the following is/are correct regarding the staffing needs for formal fine dining?**

    (1) There should be 1 maitre d' per 8 front waiters.
    (2) There should be 1 dishwasher per 2 servers and cooks.

    A. (1) only
    B. (2) only
    C. All of the above
    D. None of the above

184. **Which of the following is/are correct regarding the staffing needs for off-site catering?**

    (1) There should be 1 server per 15 customers for a reception.
    (2) There should be 1 cook per 25 to 30 customers for a reception.

    A. (1) only
    B. (2) only
    C. All of the above
    D. None of the above

185. **Which of the following is/are correct regarding the staffing needs for off-site catering?**

    (1) There should be 1 server per 3 buffet tables.
    (2) There should be 1 server per 2 tables for plated meals.

    A. (1) only
    B. (2) only
    C. All of the above
    D. None of the above

186. Determine payroll costs as a percentage of food and beverage income if the total payroll costs were $11,274 and food and beverage income was $44,398.

A. 25.39%
B. 30.44%
C. 35.21%
D. 40.83%

187. Which of the following lists the four stages of the hiring process in the correct order?

A. Recruiting, interviewing, hiring, orientation
B. Interviewing, recruiting, hiring, orientation
C. Recruiting, interviewing, orientation, hiring
D. Interviewing, hiring, orientation, recruiting

188. All but which of the following are among the three leading methods used to retain staff?

A. Adequate compensation
B. Flexible hours
C. Advancement opportunity
D. Training

189. The largest expense in a typical food and beverage operation is supplies. The second largest expense is payroll.

True
False

190. Food and beverage purchasing is generally based on a _____ system.

A. First-in-first-out
B. Quota
C. Bid
D. Last-in-last-out

191. In a successful food and beverage operation, as much as _____ of the total food and beverage budget will be spent on food purchases.

    A. 10%
    B. 40%
    C. 60%
    D. 90%

192. Which of the following terms refers to the predetermined quantities of food items the Food and Beverage Director wants to have on hand at all times?

    A. Common stock
    B. Preferred stock
    C. Par stock
    D. Average stock

193. Two reasons why it is important to maintain proper storeroom control are to avoid deterioration and prevent theft.

    True
    False

194. Which of the following inventory management methods is commonly used in a well-maintained storeroom?

    A. FIFO
    B. LIFO
    C. Average cost
    D. Specific identification

195. The four criteria for a well-maintained storeroom are proper temperature, humidity, sanitation, and air circulation.

    True
    False

196. Which of the following individuals is responsible for receiving and processing food and beverage purchase invoices?

  A. Head Professional
  B. Director of Golf
  C. Food and Beverage Director
  D. Head Waiter

197. Which of the following is/are correct regarding dram shop laws?

  (1) Dram shop laws hold a liquor-serving establishment liable for the actions of its customers.
  (2) Dram shop laws were written to increase alcohol sales.

  A. (1) only
  B. (2) only
  C. All of the above
  D. None of the above

198. Dram shop laws encourage restaurant and bar operators to use sound judgment when serving alcohol.

  True
  False

199. According to the bid system, a liquor-serving establishment may purchase alcohol from a retail store instead of a licensed vendor.

  True
  False

200. All but which of the following are correct regarding alcohol service in a golf facility?

  A. Empty liquor bottles cannot be refilled.
  B. Liquor cannot be watered down.
  C. The liquor license must be on premise but is not required to be displayed.
  D. Drinks may not be pre-mixed.

ANSWER KEY

1. B

An open-to-buy (OTB) plan helps a golf professional determine how much money should be spent on merchandise classifications, and also tracks how much money will remain each month to buy or restock inventory.

2. C

Small golf shops typically have at least 10 merchandise classifications. Large golf shops have 20 or more merchandise classifications.

3. False

In an OTB plan, approximately 10% to 25% of all dollars should be uncommitted to allow for flexibility and periodic changes in purchasing.

4. False

Cost of goods sold is the wholesale price vendors charge for merchandise. It includes merchandise that is lost or stolen.

5. True

Cost of goods sold may include additional costs such as shipping, ticketing, and handling.

6. A

COGS = beginning of month inventory + purchases – end of month inventory

7. B

COGS = $40,000 + $50,000 - $70,000
COGS = $20,000

8. False

Cost of goods sold as a percentage of sales should be between 50% and 60% for soft goods, and between 65% and 75% for hard goods.

9. A

Goods that are immediately consumed in one use are considered soft goods.

10. B
The higher a golf shop's inventory turnover rate, the less inventory is needed on hand to reach the same sales goals.

11. C
Average monthly inventory level = annual COGS / turnover rate

12. D
Average monthly inventory level = ($20,000 x 12) / 2.5
Average monthly inventory level = $96,000

13. B
The average turnover rate for all golf shops is 1.5. The average turnover rate for private equity PGA facilities is 2.5.

14. C
The average turnover rate for all sporting retailers is 3.6. The average turnover rate for top golf merchandisers is 4.0.

15. False
The highest turnover items at both private and municipal golf facilities are golf balls and shirts.

16. True
An excessively high turnover rate can lead to a higher cost of goods sold percentage.

17. B
Inventory levels should increase two months before the peak season begins. Enough inventory should be on hand at the beginning of the season to cover sales for approximately 90 days.

18. D
A merchandise assortment plan (MAP) establishes the quantity, sizes, colors, materials, models, styles, types of brands, and planned price points for each product line.

19. True
The MAP process includes reviewing the needs of customers, evaluating previous year performance by merchandise classification, researching market trends, and selecting the merchandise mix to purchase.

20. C
Anticipation dating involves setting a future date when payment is due, and offering a discount for early payment.

21.A
If a golf shop receives merchandise in the fall of the current year, with payment due in April or May of the following year, spring dating is being used.

22.A
The advantages to using extended billing strategies are the opportunity to sell items at no immediate cost, and a reduced number of back orders.

23. False
Successful golf shops concentrate their buying power with few vendors in order to improve efficiency and receive individual attention.

24. D
The Mill River Plan is often used at private facilities, and involves members paying an initial fee at the beginning of the season which allows them to purchase merchandise at a small percentage above cost.

25.A
The keystoning markup approach doubles an item's cost to arrive at the final retail price.

26. C
The cost plus markup approach uses a target markup percentage as the basis for pricing merchandise.

27. B
The keystoning markup approach doubles an item's cost to arrive at the final retail price.
$85 x 2 = $170

28. B
If a golf shop sets merchandise prices according to the manufacturer's suggested retail price, the golf shop will usually lower the price of hard goods before lowering the price of soft goods.

29. D
The competitive factors that influence price markup are exclusivity, follow the leader, opportunistic pricing, and supply and demand. Convenience is a value added factor.

30. C
The value added factors that influence price markup are product availability, facility image, services, and convenience. Supply and demand are competitive factors.

31. D
Poor turnover, not excessive turnover, is a consequence of poor pricing.

32. C
A purchase order (PO) is used to identify what merchandise is on order, when it was ordered, who ordered it, and when it will be delivered.

33. B
Markup % = markup / cost

34. D
Markup % = $18 / $26
Markup % = 69%

35. C
Gross margin % = $12 / $44
Gross margin % = 27%

36. True
When pricing merchandise, a golf professional should establish gross margin goals first, and then determine what the product markup should be in order to achieve it.

37. A
A golf facility's actual gross margin will be less than markup because some items will be marked down, lost, stolen, or damaged.

38. C
Total revenue per round = $80,000 / 1,300
Total revenue per round = $61.54

39. A
$80,000 x 0.20 = $16,000
Merchandise revenue per round = $16,000 / 1,300
Merchandise revenue per round = $12.31

40. True
Supply and demand are competitive factors that affect a golf shop's pricing strategy.

41. C
A planogram is a golf shop floor plan that illustrates where different types of merchandise should be placed.

42. False
There are six elements involved in creating an attractive buying environment for customers. They are signage, lighting, staff selling skills, fixtures, floor layout, and attention-getting displays.

43. False
Departmentalizing a golf shop is part of an effective floor layout.

44. True
Attention-getting displays in a golf shop create changing elevations, highlight a coordinated look, and make merchandise easily accessible.

45. B
When hanging merchandise, size items from left to right, beginning with the smallest size and increasing size as you move to the right.

46. A
When displaying folded merchandise, size items from top to bottom, beginning with the smallest size and increasing size as you move to the bottom.

47. True
Flexible fixtures should present older merchandise in a new light, keep the golf shop looking full when inventory is low, and enhance the golf shop's image.

48. D
A POS system automatically updates a golf shop's open-to-buy plan, allows for timely reporting of sales information, helps with price control, and maintains an accurate inventory.

49. True
"Destination items" are products that customers intend to purchase before entering the golf shop.

50. D
A golf professional should clean displays and mirrors, vacuum the floor, and organize the counter area daily. He or she should organize the back room, wipe down shelves, and clean air vents weekly.

51. C
The six steps of event preparation in the correct order are: set objectives, establish a budget, decide requirements, identify tasks, schedule activities, and communicate the plan.

52. False
The five steps of the selling process in the correct order are: approach the customer, collect key information, present merchandise, close the sale, and build future sales.

53. B
A physical inventory count should be performed at least twice per year.

54. True
A perpetual book inventory system tracks changes to merchandise levels, both in terms of dollar value and number of units, on a daily basis or as they occur.

55. False
Financial value inventory tracking indicates the dollar value of inventory on hand and sold, and the history of price changes and markdowns.

56. D
Physical unit inventory tracking indicates the quantity of merchandise on hand, sold, and on order, and the age of the merchandise.

57. A
Advantages of high merchandise turnover include fewer markdowns, better ROI, and an increased ability to capitalize on new trends. Higher cost of goods sold percentage is a potential disadvantage of high turnover.

58. B
The gross profit margin for a public golf facility should be at least 30%. The gross profit margin for a private golf facility should be at least 50%.

59. C
Inventory turnover rate = $83,250 / $51,400
Inventory turnover rate = 1.62

60. A
Average inventory at cost = total end of month inventory on hand / length of season

61. True
Gross margin return on investment (GMROI) calculates the profit made for each dollar spent on inventory.

62. False
Golf shops that achieve a GMROI of 110% to 160% are considered to be performing very well.

63. True
Gross margin is defined as the difference between total merchandise sales and the cost of goods sold.

64. C
Gross margin return on investment (GMROI) allows a golf professional to measure the true profitability of different products, such as those that have high margins (golf shoes) and those that have high turnover (golf tees).

65. D
To successfully manage a golf shop, a golf professional should track sales performance, analyze variances in sales, and adjust factors as needed.

66. False
Point-of-sale markdowns are temporary markdowns, and typically take place during special events. Permanent markdowns are permanent reductions in list price and should be indicated on merchandise tags.

67. C
Delegating is a partnership building process that empowers employees.

68. False
Delegating is a partnership building process, not a technique used to control employees.

69. D
Two key factors a manager should consider before delegating an assignment to an employee are capabilities and willingness.

70. B
The "involving" interaction strategy should be used by a manager if an employee is resistant and experienced.

71. A
The "directing" interaction strategy should be used by a manager if an employee is enthusiastic and inexperienced.

72. D
The "supporting" interaction strategy should be used by a manager if an employee is enthusiastic and experienced.

73. C
The "convincing" interaction strategy should be used by a manager if an employee is resistant and inexperienced.

74. C
Resources are the basic means available to an employee in completing a task.

75. A
Input is the information, circumstances, or events that prompt an employee to take action to complete a task.

76. C
Feedback is the specific information an employee receives about the results of his or her actions.

77. D
The building blocks to creating motivating work are the performer, the work assignment, and the work environment.

78. C
The five principles of motivating work are skill variety, whole task, significant work, autonomy, and feedback.

79. B
The five principles of motivating work are skill variety, whole task, significant work, autonomy, and feedback.

80. True
Autonomy is allowing staff members to decide how best to complete a task.

81. False
The statement refers to "whole task", not autonomy.

82. D
An input amplifier makes a manager's input even more obvious and understandable.

83. C
The "whole task" principle of motivating work is being used when a manager reorganizes tasks around natural and complete units of work.

84. D
The "significant work" principle of motivating work is being used when a manager looks for opportunities to build into a job the type of work an employee wants to do.

85. False
Four ways a manager can make performance problems worse are inaction, wrong assumptions, failure to involve the employee, and missed opportunities.

86. B
The first stage of the four-stage sequence for correcting performance problems is "joint problem solving with the performer".

87. A
The second stage of the four-stage sequence for correcting performance problems is "reinforced problem solving with the performer".

88. D
The third stage of the four-stage sequence for correcting performance problems is "final decision making with the performer".

89. C
The fourth stage of the four-stage sequence for correcting performance problems is "termination of the employment relationship".

90. B
The manager will insist on the need to resolve the performance problem, and re-emphasize the importance of the performer's role in the resolution process in Stage 2 (reinforced problem solving with the performer) of the four-stage sequence for correcting performance problems.

91. A
The "directing" strategy is most likely to be used in Stage 3 (final decision making with the performer) of the four-stage sequence for correcting performance problems.

92. A
The manager will ask the employee for ideas on how to solve a performance-based problem in Stage 1 (joint problem solving with the performer) of the four-stage sequence for correcting performance problems.

93. C

A teaching philosophy summarizes an instructor's views, beliefs, concepts, and attitudes towards the game of golf and how it should be taught. A teaching philosophy is essentially an instructor's mission statement.

94. D

Harry Vardon is famously quoted as saying, "Putting is the game within a game."

95. False

Putting strokes account for approximately 43% of all strokes taken during a round of golf for a low handicap player.

96. True

Proper putting technique suggests a golfer's eye line should be directly over, or slightly inside, the ball.

97. B

The reverse overlap is the most common putting grip.

98. C

The goals of selecting the proper putting grip are to resist wristiness and resist clubface rotation.

99. False

For the proper putting setup, the ball should be forward of center and the eye line should be directly over the ball.

100. True

The average loft of a putter is 4.0 degrees, and the average lie is 73.5 degrees. The average putter length is 35.5 inches, and the average weight is 11.5 ounces.

101. C

For long distance putts, the goal is to have the next putt be 3 feet or less.

102. A

Bermudagrass has the most grain.

103. B

A shiny putting surface means the grain is going away from the golfer. A dull surface means the grain is going towards the golfer.

104. C
60% of a putt's break will occur within three feet of the hole. Grain usually affects only the last foot of role.

105. A
X-out golf balls are poorly balanced for putting, and can affect a 6-foot putt by as many as 3 or 4 inches. A 2.5 foot putt has an alignment error of +/- 4 degrees.

106. False
The distinguishing factor between a chip and a pitch is that a pitch is a two-lever stroke (cocked wrists), and a chip is a one-lever stroke (firm wrists).

107. True
The preferred method of transitioning from chipping to pitching is moving the ball to the centerline of the body using a wedge.

108. A
When chipping and pitching, grip pressure may be firm or light, but should never be tight. Firmer grip pressure slows clubhead speed, and lighter grip pressure increases it.

109. D
The feet and hips should be open when chipping and pitching in order to restrict the backswing for greater control.

110. B
When chipping and pitching from a bare lie, move the ball back in stance. For a fluffy lie move the ball forward in stance.

111. A
When chipping and pitching, move the ball forward in stance to produce a higher trajectory. Move the ball back in stance to produce a lower trajectory.

112. False
The vertical centerline of a golfer's body should be 2 inches in front of the ball for a chip, and even for a pitch.

113. True
A useful phrase to recite when teaching the principles of chipping and pitching is, "The left hand should never stop moving towards the target."

114. D
To hit a cut shot, aim left, open the clubface, keep the hands and arms back, and move the body forward.

115. True
To hit a cut-lob shot, move the ball forward in stance, open the clubface, and swing with the arms.

116. D
To hit a flop shot, allow the left wrist to break downward, strike the ball with a steep descent, and maintain wristy action through the golf ball.

117. A
A sand wedge has camber, sole inversion, and breadth to help easily remove the ball from a greenside bunker.

118. C
Camber is the curvature of a golf club's sole.

119. B
Breadth is the width of a golf club's sole.

120. B
Gene Sarazan is credited with inventing the modern sand wedge.

121. B
For greenside bunker shots, bounce is promoted if the heel of the golf club leads. Dig is promoted if the toe of the golf club leads.

122. B
Camber helps irons dig less into the ground when taking divots. Camber is the curvature of a golf club's sole.

123. True
Sole inversion is caused by the bottom of a golf club's sole being lower than the leading edge.

124. B
To play a buried greenside bunker shot, the ball should be further back in stance to increase penetration with the clubface. Turn the toe of the clubhead in for a knife-like leading edge to penetrate through the sand more easily.

125.A

For bunker shots, a steep angle of approach will make the ball travel a shorter a distance than a shallow angle of approach with the same effort.

126.A

For a greenside bunker shot, the ball should be played 4 to 6 inches left of the golfer's vertical centerline.

127. False

For a greenside bunker shot, a "V" shaped swing will produce a higher and softer shot. A "U" shaped swing will hit the ball lower and further with the same effort.

128. False

Always contact the ball first when hitting from a fairway bunker.

129. True

As a rule of thumb, a golfer should choke down on the club as far down as his feet are buried into the sand for a fairway bunker shot.

130. B

For fairway bunker shots, firm sand requires less bounce. Soft sand requires more bounce.

131. True

"Balancing a glass of water on the clubface" is a useful visual image to teach students in order to keep them from closing the clubface during greenside bunker shots.

132. C

For a sidehill lie with the ball above the feet, a golfer's tendency will be to chunk, pull, or hook the ball.

133.A

For a sidehill lie with the ball above the feet, the golfer should stand as perpendicular to the lie as possible.

134.A

For a sidehill lie with the ball below the feet, a golfer's tendency will be to push, slice, or top the ball.

135. D

For an uphill lie, a golfer's tendency will be to chunk, pull, or hit behind the ball.

136. False

For an uphill lie, the golfer should lean into the hill in order to resist gravity's pull.

137. False

When playing a golf shot into the wind, the golfer should try to minimize backspin so the ball doesn't upshoot. For this reason, a punch shot into the wind is not recommended.

138. B

For a downhill lie, a golfer's tendency will be to top, push, or hit behind the ball.

139. False

To hook the golf ball, sole the clubface square and use a closed face grip. Aim the feet and shoulders to the right of the target.

140. A

A semi-private teaching lesson includes 2 to 4 students.

141. True

A group lesson should be limited to 5 to 12 students in total. This allows 3 to 5 minutes each for individual instruction.

142. B

A participation clinic includes a blend of demonstration, observation, and coaching students while they hit golf balls.

143. A

The purpose of a demonstration clinic is to educate and entertain students by blending fun with fundamentals.

144. False

A demonstration clinic should be limited to 45 minutes if the audience is seated.

145. B

When hosting a golf school, the maximum student-teacher ratio should not exceed 8 to 1.

146. B

The three basic body types are endomorph, ectomorph, and mesomorph.

147. D

An endomorph is characterized by small bones, low muscle tone, and a frame that is soft and round. Individuals with this body type are generally poor athletes.

148. A
An ectomorph is characterized by thin muscles, thin bones, a short trunk, and long arms and legs. Individuals with this body type generally have high endurance levels.

149. C
A mesomorph is characterized by large muscles, big bones, broad shoulders, and a slender waist. Individuals with this body type generally have increased strength.

150. False
Golfers who are short in stature generally have good balance, a flat swing, a shallow angle of approach, and tend to draw the ball.

151. True
Senior golfers who are losing strength and range of motion should adopt a more clockwise-positioned grip to reduce forearm and hand rotation.

152. False
Although having fun is an important aspect of junior golf, it is the responsibility of the PGA Professional to teach history, traditions, rules, and etiquette. Rules and etiquette are important safety elements as well.

153. B
The ideal ages to learn the golf swing are between 13 and 20 years old.

154. True
While 10% to 15% of Americans are left-handed, only 3% to 6% play golf left-handed.

155. True
A right-handed golf instructor should use himself as a mirror image when teaching swing fundamentals to a left-handed student.

156. D
The four basic components that affect a golfer's skill level are strength, flexibility, muscular endurance, and cardiovascular endurance.

157. True
A successful food and beverage operation should be flexible and follow the acronym PACE, which stands for primary plan, alternative plan, contingency plan, and emergency plan.

158. A
An example of an objective in the food and beverage industry is to establish and grow profit for the long-term. Strategies are the steps required to connect tangible actions with intangible objectives.

159. C
Food cost control means following the golf facility's predetermined standards, while exercising restraint over the price the facility pays to purchase, prepare, and sell food.

160. False
Food cost control can be applied to areas such as purchasing, receiving, service, storeroom, and menu.

161. A
At least 50% of a golf facility's non-dues related income should come from food and beverage operations.

162. True
The primary goal of successful food and beverage operations is to achieve total customer satisfaction.

163. D
The three basic types of golf facilities are public, private, and semi-private.

164. C
The three basic types of private golf facilities are developer-owned, equity, and privately managed.

165. B
An equity golf facility is owned by its members. Service, not profit, is the operational goal.

166. D
A privately managed golf facility has high profit and full membership as its primary goals.

167. False
There are six levels of food and beverage service in the golf industry. They are on-course concessions, carryout, full service, formal fine dining, banquets, and off-site catering.

168. A
The easiest and least expensive level of food and beverage service is on-course concessions because it requires minimal staff and equipment.

169. B

The menu is the most basic and important control tool used in a food and beverage operation.

170. C

The four steps of menu development in the correct order are: develop the menu concept, develop and test recipes, determine menu costs, and print the menu and train staff.

171. B

A standard recipe is the blueprint used to develop a food and beverage item.

172. True

A "picture board" should be maintained in the kitchen to demonstrate the standard plate presentation.

173. C

The Food and Beverage Director should cost all menu items quarterly to ensure they remain within budgeted goals.

174. A

Standard portion cost = total cost of recipe / number of portions

175. B

Standard portion cost = $440 / 40
Standard portion cost = $11

176. True

To determine a menu item's base selling price, multiply the entrée cost by the price multiplier. The price multiplier is equal to 100% divided by the food cost goal.

177. D

100 / 28 = 3.57
$2.95 x 3.57 = $10.53

178. C

The goal of identifying appropriate staffing levels for a food and beverage operation is to balance customer service with payroll efficiency.

179. C

For on-course concessions, there should be 1 attendant per 50 to 60 rounds of golf. For carryout service, there should be 1 attendant per 20 to 30 rounds of golf per hour.

180. False
For a full service food and beverage operation, there should be 1 server and cook per 12 customers per hour. There should be 1 bartender/washer/host/busser per 5 to 6 servers.

181. C
For formal fine dining, there should be 1 cook per 10 customers.

182. D
For formal fine dining, there should be 1 front server per 12 customers.

183. B
For formal fine dining, there should be 1 maitre d' per 4 front waiters. There should be 1 dishwasher per 2 servers and cooks.

184. B
For off-site catering, there should be 1 server per 30 customers for a reception. There should be 1 cook per 25 to 30 customers for a reception.

185. C
For off-site catering, there should be 1 server per 3 buffet tables. There should be 1 server per 2 tables for plated meals.

186. A
$11,274 / $44,398 = 25.39%

187. A
The four stages of the hiring process in the correct order are: recruiting, interviewing, hiring, and orientation.

188. B
The three leading methods used to retain staff are adequate compensation, advancement opportunity, and training.

189. False
The largest expense in a typical food and beverage operation is payroll. The second largest expense is supplies.

190. C
Food and beverage purchasing is generally based on a bid system.

191. B

In a successful food and beverage operation, as much as 40% of the total food and beverage budget will be spent on food purchases.

192. C

Par stock refers to the predetermined quantities of food items the Food and Beverage Director wants to have on hand at all times.

193. True

Two reasons why it is important to maintain proper storeroom control are to avoid deterioration and prevent theft.

194. A

Well-maintained storerooms commonly use the FIFO (first-in-first-out) inventory management method.

195. True

The four criteria for a well-maintained storeroom are proper temperature, humidity, sanitation, and air circulation.

196. C

The Food and Beverage Director is responsible for receiving and processing food and beverage purchase invoices.

197. A

Dram shop laws hold a liquor-serving establishment liable for the actions of its customers.

198. True

Dram shop laws encourage restaurant and bar operators to use sound judgment when serving alcohol.

199. False

A liquor-serving establishment must purchase liquor from a licensed vendor.

200. C

The liquor license must be displayed at all times.

ABOUT THE AUTHORS

Ryan Brandeburg is a PGA member and serves as the Director of Golf for The Lodge at Kauri Cliffs and The Farm at Cape Kidnappers on the North Island of New Zealand. Both golf courses consistently rank among the top 50 in the world, and Ryan's responsibilities include managing the daily operations and strategic direction for each course. Ryan has an extensive background in private and resort operations, and has formerly served as the Acting Director of Golf at Waldorf Astoria Golf Club in Orlando, Florida, and the Head Golf Professional at Naples Grande Golf Club in Naples, Florida.

Matthew Brandeburg is a certified financial planner and President of Bridgeway Financial Group, LLC in Columbus, Ohio. Matthew is the author of the books "Financial Planning For Your First Job", "Your Guide to the CFP Certification Exam", "CFP Certification Exam Practice Question Workbook", and "PGA Professional Golf Management Practice Question Workbook". He is also the creator of the mobile apps "Investment Allocator" and "Pocket Financial Planner". In addition, Matthew teaches the class "Financial Planning in your 20s and 30s" at Ohio State University.

INDEX